The Best of Coaching Volleyball, Book I:
The Basic Elements of the Game

Edited by Kinda Asher

MASTERS PRESS

A Division of Howard W. Sams & Co.

Published by Masters Press
A Division of Howard W. Sams & Co.
2647 Waterfront Pkwy. E. Dr., Suite 300
Indianapolis, IN 46214

Published 1995

Printed in the United States of America

Library of Congress Cataloging-in-Publication Data

The best of coaching volleyball series of handbooks / American Volleyball Coaches Association.
    p.   cm.
  Includes bibliographical references and indexes.
  Contents: [1] Basic elements of the game -- [2] Advanced elements of the game -- [3] Related elements of the game.
    ISBN 1-570238-083-5 (v.1). -- ISBN 1-57028-08403 (v.2). -- ISBN 1-57028-085-1 (v.3).
    1. Volleyball --Coaching--Handbooks, manuals, etc. I. American Volleyball Coaches Association. II. Coaching volleyball.

GV1015.5.C63B47   1995   95-43827
796.325--dc20   CIP

10 9 8 7 6 5 4 3   97 98 99 00

The Best of Coaching Volleyball, Book I: The Basic Elements of the Game

Credits:

Cover design by Suzanne Lincoln
Text design by Kevin Kaneshiro, American Volleyball Coaches Association
Cover photo by Judy Sondermann

Table of Contents

Contributors

Authors

Iradge Ahrabi-Fard, Ph.D., head women's coach, University of Northern Iowa (Cedar Falls, Iowa)

Horst Baacke, Federation Internationale de Volleyball (FIVB) technical advisor

Doug Beal, Ph.D., special assistant to the executive director/CEO, USA Volleyball

Nick Cheronis, assistant women's coach, University of Florida (Gainesville, Fla.)

Sandra Collins, head girls' coach, Bethlehem High School (Delmar, N.Y.)

Kathy DeBoer, associate athletics director, University of Kentucky (Lexington, Ky.)

*Steve DeBoer, former assistant women's coach, College of William & Mary (Williamsburg, Va.); now resides in Columbus, Ohio

Tim Davison, head girls' coach, Yakima Valley Elite (Yakima, Wash.)

Mashallah Farokhmanesh, assistant women's coach, Washington State University (Pullman, Wash.)

Dorothy Franco-Reed, head women's coach, University of Alabama (Tuscaloosa, Ala.)

Cathy George, head women's coach, Western Michigan University (Kalamazoo, Mich.)

Bernie Goldfine, Ph.D., associate professor, Kennesaw State College, Marietta, Ga.

Zen Golembiowsky, Hinckley, Ohio

Jerry Gregg, head girls' coach, Cypress High School (Cypress, Calif.)

Karen Guthmiller, athletics director, Lee College (Baytown, Texas)

Sharon Huddleston, Ph.D., professor, University of Northern Iowa (Cedar Falls, Iowa)

Thomas Keating, head girls' coach, Wahlert High School (Dubuque, Iowa)

Geri Knortz, head women's coach, Hamilton College (Clinton, N.Y.)

Lisa Love, head women's coach, University of Southern California (Los Angeles, Calif.)

Sean Madden, head women's coach, Gonzaga University (Spokane, Wash.)

M. Eileen Mathews, head girls' coach, East Valley School District (Yakima, Wash.)

Carl McGown, Ph.D., head men's coach, Brigham Young University (Provo, Utah)

*Lois Mueller, Ed.D., former head women's coach, Concordia

University (Mequon, Wis.)

Bill Neville, head women's coach, University of Washington (Seattle, Wash.)

Dave Orren, head women's coach, University of St. Thomas (St. Thomas, Minn.)

Tom Pingel, head girls' coach, Circle City Volleyball club (Indianapolis, Ind.)

Joan Powell, head girls' coach, Coronado High School (Colorado Springs, Colo.)

*Stephanie Schleuder, former head women's coach, University of Minnesota (Minneapolis, Minn.)

Don Shondell, Ph.D., head men's coach, Ball State University (Muncie, Ind.)

Mary Ann Sprague, head girls' coach, Jacksonville Juniors Volleyball Club (Jacksonville, Fla.)

*Peter John Stefaniuk, head men's coach, George Brown College of Applied Arts and Technology (Toronto, Ontario, Canada)

Editors

General Editor: Kinda Asher, director of publications, American Volleyball Coaches Association

Copy Editors: Sandra Vivas and Vivian Langley

Advisors

Darlene Kluka, Ph.D., assistant professor, University of Central Oklahoma

Geri Polvino, Ph.D., head women's coach, Eastern Kentucky University

Don Shondell, Ph.D., head men's coach, Ball State University

Sandra Vivas, executive director, American Volleyball Coaches Association

*coaching position at the time the article was first published in *Coaching Volleyball*.

Acknowledgements

KINDA ASHER

In today's world, the measure of true success is seen in the compilation. Professional musicians release "best of" CDs, while actors and actresses are judged by the body of their work, as are authors and researchers. Indeed, if a particular person, event or publication has been around long enough — and has been successful enough — to warrant a "collection," there is a demand for the product. Since 1987, there has been a demand for *Coaching Volleyball*, the official technical journal of the American Volleyball Coaches Association, and now the best the publication has to offer can be found in a new series of books.

The *Best of Coaching Volleyball* series (Books I-III) was the brainchild of the *Coaching Volleyball* Editorial Board and the AVCA office staff. The AVCA is continually searching for innovative avenues to serve its members from an educational standpoint; the *Best of Coaching Volleyball* series is one of the many innovations.

The project could not have begun without the Editorial Board, specifically Darlene Kluka, Ph.D. (assistant professor, University of Central Oklahoma), Geri Polvino, Ph.D. (head women's volleyball coach, Eastern Kentucky) and Don Shondell, Ph.D. (head men's volleyball coach, Ball State University), without whose expertise and patience this publication would have floundered. In addition, the AVCA membership itself must be praised, as it is the members of the organization — the coaches of all levels — who provide the articles for *Coaching Volleyball* on a consistent basis. Without their willingness to share ideas on this ever changing sport, the journal itself would not exist. The coaches who are also USA Volleyball Coaching Accreditation Program (CAP) members strive continually to "shake up" the volleyball world with innovative new techniques and tactics.

Undeniably, the heartiest thanks must go to the 32 coaches whose works appear in this publication. Revisions and fine tuning of these articles was a responsibility thrust upon them — and each took the challenge to heart.

Finally, many thanks go to Tom Bast, publisher, Holly Kondras, editor, and the rest of the Masters Press staff for their support and expertise throughout the varied stages of this project.

Kinda S. Asher
AVCA Director of Publications
October 1995

Preface

KINDA ASHER

Eight years ago, the American Volleyball Coaches Association recognized the need for a technical journal specifically designed for volleyball coaches of all levels, from junior/club to international. As a result, *Coaching Volleyball* was born.

Today, *Coaching Volleyball* serves as the leading periodical devoted to the technical aspects of the game. The journal is read bi-monthly by more than 3,000 AVCA members and subscribers, both domestic and international. The demand for technically correct information on coaching and learning the sport has inspired the AVCA to compile the best articles from the technical journal and showcase them in a series of three publications. The *Best of Coaching Volleyball* series (Books I-III) is the response to that need.

In this, the first book of the series, novice coaches and players are treated to 27 chapters discussing the basic elements of the game of volleyball. Coaches from all levels -- and from all around the country-- offer their ideas on how to teach the serve, the attack, the set, etc. It is truly an eclectic combination of information geared to the up-and-coming young coach or player.

The book is divided into eight sections:

Section I	Establishing a Solid Volleyball Program
Section II	The Serve
Section III	The Set
Section IV	The Attack
Section V	The Block
Section VI	Serve Receive
Section VII	Defense
Section VIII	How to Develop Drills

Thirty-two coaches have offered their varied expertise on the sport of volleyball. Each chapter is rife with photos, graphics and diagrams to aid the reader in understanding and grasping the material. In addition, a number of the chapters pull related information from other sources to provide the reader with an even broader base of information. Indeed, the *Best of Coaching Volleyball* series is unlike any volleyball publication you have read.

Kinda Asher

Section I: Establishing a Solid Volleyball Program

Establishing and Maintaining
Excellence in a High School
Volleyball Program

Establishing and Maintaining Excellence in a High School Volleyball Program

Thomas Keating

Set your performance and behavior expectations high for all of your players.

Why do some high school volleyball programs flourish, some flirt with success, some soak in mediocrity and others fail? How can you turn your program around and enjoy the success that so many coaches envy? The answer is commitment. Coaches with flourishing programs have committed themselves to excellence. They spend the time, effort and energy necessary to keep ahead of the competition.

How did they do it? Where did they start? Most successful coaches started where you are now. You can do the same! Following are what I consider the seven keys to establishing and maintaining excellence in a high school volleyball program.

SETTING GOALS IS A MUST

The first step in achieving anything is to set goals. Setting goals is like planning a trip. Without either process, you have no idea of where you want to get, let alone how to get there. A sense of direction is one of the most important ingredients in the excellence recipe.

Goal setting time must be scheduled. Coaches must allot time for setting their own goals, for the team to set goals together and for players to set personal goals. Daily goals, match goals, weekly goals and season goals all have a place in the high-level program. The time used to give yourself, your team and your players direction is time well-spent.

> Athletes can always play without a coach. No one can coach without players.

The type of goal set will determine to a great extent its value. Goals should be measurable. Coaches and players should be able to answer the question, "How will I know when I have accomplished my goal?" An example of a goal that is difficult to measure would be, "Serve tough." A measurable goal relating to the same concept might be "Serve at least 2.0 (on a 3.0 scale)."

Goals should be evaluated regularly. Have players hand in daily goals at the beginning of practice. At the end of practice, have them write one or two comments about how they felt they did on that goal. At weekly goal sessions, we evaluate the previous week's goals before we set the next week's goals.

Setting goals for different areas of volleyball and different areas of the players' lives can help give players added direction. Practice goals, tournament goals, classroom goals and relationship goals are just a few examples.

EXCELLENT PEOPLE MAKE EXCELLENT PROGRAMS

Because programs involve people, the first step in developing an excellent program is beginning with excellent people. This starts with you, the head coach. There are terrific coaches in this country—coaches who work hard and provide positive role models for their players. Unfortunately, there are also hypocrites. Some coaches demand dedication and responsible behavior from their athletes while putting in minimal time themselves or behaving in ways they deem unacceptable for their play-

Photo: USM

Videotaping players and discussing the results can have great impact on how they perform a certain skill.

According to Steve Nimocks in his article "Random Thoughts on Improving a High School Volleyball Program" (*Coaching Volleyball*, December/January 1993), you can cultivate a strong base of athletes through your junior high feeder schools. In fact, "many high school head coaches are officially "in charge" of the program within their junior highs, as well as the high school. Even if not, many junior high coaches will welcome your input. For example, decide what footwork you want your players to use and teach it to your junior high coaches, as well as your players" (p. 11).

ers. Remember, players hear best with their eyes. What they see is what you will get.

Expect much from yourself. Develop your coaching skills by attending clinics and college practices. Offer to help at summer volleyball camps run by successful coaches. Meet your responsibilities. Be the first one to arrive at practice and the last one to leave. Take care of equipment. Call in your scores to the local media. Turn in necessary forms to your athletic director. Improve your relationships with others. Be cooperative and friendly toward opposing coaches and officials. Learn to talk with your players and their parents. Make sure you practice what you preach. Keep control of yourself.

You should expect the same of your assistant coaches. Encourage them to strive for the same standards you have set for yourself. It is important to recognize their contributions to the program. Monitor your assistants. If they are not following your program's guidelines, discuss it. Remember, you will be dealing on the varsity level with the player attitudes and skill levels that your assistant coaches helped develop a few years before.

Of course, the most important ingredient of any program is its players. Athletes can always play without a coach. No one can coach without players. An excellent program, then, must have players who are excellent people.

Players, like most people, behave as expected. If you expect Cindy to be a real troublemaker, she will probably oblige. We often give subtle hints to our players about how we expect them to behave and perform. (How many players labeled "lazy" act any differently?) Set your performance and behavior expectations high.

One thing we learned is that players cannot differentiate their behavior on and off the court. If they are easily distracted in the classroom, they will be easily distracted on the volleyball court. Those who are discourteous to students and teachers will be discourteous to coaches, officials and teammates. By the same token, if they are positive off the court (responsible, competitive, cooperative), they will make a valuable contribution to the team.

Expose your players to positive role models. Ask former players, now respected adults, to talk to your team. Take your players to college matches. Show them videos of motivational speakers.

Your players must want to play. Usually a coach comes to regret begging someone to play on a team. That player will feel that she has the upper hand—and the coach may feel he or she owes that player something. It is not good for either one.

EXCELLENCE IS A LONG-TERM PROCESS

Establishing excellence in a program takes time. It will not happen overnight. The sooner a coach accepts this fact, the easier it will be to focus on long-term goals, which are the key to establishing excellence. For example, our first state title came in my fourth year at Wahlert High School. But it was in the first year that my assistants and I set long-range plans toward that end.

Many high school teams can have "sudden success." A school may have one or more great athletes in a class and enjoy tremendous success during their careers. Often, though, when those athletes graduate, the success leaves with them. Excellent programs distinguish themselves from temporary winners and maintain a winning tradition by establishing a talent pool for the varsity program.

It takes organization and a willingness to work to develop a talent pool. During the season you, as head coach, need to focus on and work with your varsity squad. Your younger players are under the tutelage of your assistant and the sophomore, freshman and junior high coaches. Each coach should know your expectations and should be doing things similarly, albeit at a more fundamental level. Occasional meetings can help ensure that this goal is met.

Remember, we are not born with the knowledge that makes us successful - we must learn it.

During the off-season work with the younger players in your program. Set up clinics, workshops, camps or leagues for them. Do all you can to "turn them on" to volleyball. Many coaches take the easy way out by claiming to be victims of their players' talent. A coach who says "If I had the players she has, I would win, too" is overlooking that those players were developed somewhere by someone. Work to develop talent!

Nothing comes easily. Everyone has to work to be successful. Some programs require more building or rebuilding than others; it is important that you accurately assess your program to determine how much work needs to be done. Where are you now and where do you want to be? The further you are from your goals, the harder you will have to work.

You must commit yourself to change. Plan to spend considerable time working to improve your players and your program. Many players are willing to stay late to work on their games if they know their coach is willing to help. But coaches often give the impression that such requests infringe on their time. These players are yearning to learn—work with them! If you cannot do it after practice, meet before school begins. Many players are ready to sacrifice in order to improve.

You may want to run, for a season or two, sophomore or freshmen practices as well as your own. This ensures that everyone in your program is learning the same way. It takes a lot of time, but it is worth considering.

Showing is more effective than telling. Try to videotape your players during both practice and matches. Get close-up shots in practice and set a time to study the video with each player. It is amazing how a little graphic evidence can change a player's performance or attitude. Maybe

Linda Moulton, in her article titled "Commitment and Assistant Coaches" (*Coaching Volleyball*, April/May 1991) believes assistant coaches must be given a clear outline of job duties. "In most situations, assistant coaches are hired by the head coach, who wants a particular responsibility covered, as well as someone who can share in the daily running of the program. In some situations, the assistant may be a recent graduate who wants to continue involvement in the program. In other situations, the assistant may be carried over from the previous coach or appointed to fill a dual administrative/coaching role. Regardless the needs are the same:
- a clear understanding of what the job involves
- expectations for practices and games
- how and when evaluations will take place
- feedback.

The ability of the head coach to communicate effectively is essential to personal and professional growth of the assistant coach. Good communication can impact the overall quality of the assistant's experience and contribute to the success of the program" (p. 31).

you feel "My players are okay—it is me who needs to improve." Congratulations! You have taken the first step to improving yourself. Remember, we are not born with the knowledge that makes us successful— we must learn it. In addition to attending clinics, try a couple of these suggestions:

Watch another high school or college practice. Take notes. Go back a second, third, or fourth time. Ask questions of successful high school or college coaches. Have your manager videotape you during practice. Evaluate how you relate to your players verbally and nonverbally. Are you giving positive messages? Are you teaching? Tape record yourself during matches for the same purpose. You might be surprised at what you hear.

COACHES NEVER KNOW ENOUGH

The game of volleyball is changing too quickly for any of us to think we know enough to be successful. Jump serves, slides, combination playsets, backcourt attacks and setter attacks are just a few examples of strategies teams have burned by because coaches failed to keep up or stay ahead of trends in the game. Volleyball coaches have a lot of creative latitude because the game is still evolving. Those coaching now are inventors! What coaches create today may be tomorrow's standards. Be courageous enough to try your own ideas. Create unorthodox defenses, blocking schemes, serve receive patterns and offenses to counter opponents' strengths or take advantage of their weaknesses.

It is important that coaches be evaluated—it is sometimes the only way to realize that change is in order. I am a strong believer in evaluation from both above and below. At the end of each season our athletic director and I have at least one conference (usually more) to evaluate my performance. I also ask my players to evaluate me using a form I devised that includes an objective scale and open-ended questions. A word of caution: Do not expect all comments to be positive! Pay attention to the unsatisfactory ratings and work to improve.

EVERYONE NEEDS A CHALLENGE

Expectations affect performance. That is why most teams play better against better competition. They realize that their effort must be high.

Evaluate your schedule. Is it tough enough? Does it challenge your players? Is it helping your team prepare for postseason play? Then again, do not overload. A team that plays all tough teams and goes 0-18 is not gaining from the experience. Evaluate your talent and construct a schedule that is challenging, yet realistic.

How tough are your practices? Do your players feel pressure? The only way to prepare your team physically and mentally for competition is to provide the atmosphere at practice that they will encounter in matches. High expectations at practice result in high-quality practices. Sometimes "Nice try" should be replaced with "Get back in there and try it again."

THE QUEST FOR EXCELLENCE IS A CONTINUING PROCESS

You never really reach excellence.

It is more of a journey than a destination. You must continue to push yourself and your players to improve. When you become satisfied with where you are as a coach or a team, others will pass you by. Keep improving and it will be difficult for your opponents to see you, much less catch you!

It is easy to state your desire to establish and maintain excellence in your program, but it is difficult to achieve. It takes a commitment of time, effort and energy. Those who commit ultimately succeed. Those who find reasons why they cannot do what it takes must be satisfied with mediocrity.

Tom Keating is the head girls' volleyball coach at Wahlert High School in Dubuque, Iowa.

Tryout Testing for
High School Players

With parental pressure as powerful and destructive as it can be today, coaches must protect themselves. Documentation is imperative, especially with tryout procedures and results. Regardless of how many players come out or whether your school or district permits "cuts," a system should be implemented that fairly places athletes. Subjective evaluation, even from a coach with years of experience and impressive credentials, is just not good enough. Using your judgment alone only weakens your defense when asked by an athlete, "Why am I on JV?" or asked by a parent, "Why was my daughter cut?" Granted, some players are poor testers and great gamers, but coaches must be able to prove placement and rejection.

With an effective group of volleyball tests and measurements, others will be less likely to question your ability to cut or divide junior varsity and varsity.

Thus, for the past seven years, I have used the following battery of six physical tests and three volleyball skills tests. All tests are based on a point system; <u>skills are worth twice the physical tests.</u> I have found that the players fall into place. I have even gone so far as to put a list of names of the prospective varsity in a sealed envelope prior to the first day of practice and open the envelope in front of my staff to find no difference at the completion of testing. My "gut" feeling would never satisfy my athletes or their parents. Administrators are most appreciative when a coach enters a parent conference loaded with documented information. It is also motivating when results are posted daily and deters the "whiners from crying foul" when they return home from tryouts. At the parents' mandatory meeting prior to our first match, the daily results are posted, also.

The following is the battery of physical tests administered on Monday, Wednesday and Friday (with tests Nos. 2-6 in a rotational system) during the morning sessions of a two-week, two-a-day practice (see Figure 1).

The last two tests are subjective evaluations where the coaching staff observes team play, cooperation, competitiveness, enthusiasm, body language and attitude. These are administered on Tuesdays and Thursdays through narrow court doubles (see Figure 2) and six-on-six with wash drills (see Figure 3). Coaches make notes and meet during lunch to discuss each player's contributions and weaknesses.

PLAYER ATTITUDE

Coachability and attitude are crucial, yet coaches say they have so little time to train behavior. Coaches must take the time and build in some challenging circumstances to their drills. For instance, while running a wash drill, call a "mystery net or ball handling, just to see how a particular player deals with it. Or use what we call a "teachable moment" following a technical or mental error and replicate the scenario and have the athlete repeat the skill correctly. Or ask, "If you had a chance to do that again, what would you choose to do differently?" Coaches can get a sense of coachability during these situations. It is far better to correct behavior in practice than during a game after a yellow or red card! Too many coaches turn their heads in practice and competition so as not to cause a controversy; thus, unwanted behavior is tolerated and continued.

The rest of the players find this unfair and it will soon cause dissension. It seems the misbehavior comes from the best player and coaches who do not wish to address the problem because they "need" the player in the line-up. False! No one needs an attitude problem on their team. Confront the player in a meeting; always have another coach or athletic director with you; you do not need the conversation misinterpreted when taken home. I have found that asking the individual how you can help them become a more positive player and role model for the younger players seems to set a good tone. Listen. Set expectations. Discipline the undesirable behavior and reward the desirable behavior.

SUMMARY

In conclusion, this physical and skills testing seems to be successful. The physical testing demonstrates volleyball athleticism— agility, coordination, jumping ability and some cardiovascular endurance, even though we are interested in short, explosive spurts. The volleyball skills tests are not necessarily valid according to a tests and measurements text, but administered fairly, they can be a good indicator of a person's skill in volleyball. Players and parents seem to better understand your expectations and are less likely to question your ability to "cut" or divide JV and varsity team members. (Share your policy with your players and parents about moving up and down.) Try it and reduce your stress!

Joan Powell is the head girls' volleyball coach at Coronado High School in Colorado Springs, Colo., and is a USA Volleyball CAP certified coach.

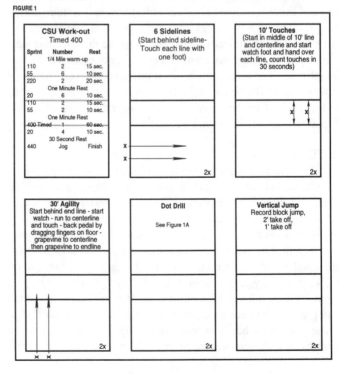

FIGURE 1

FIGURE 1a

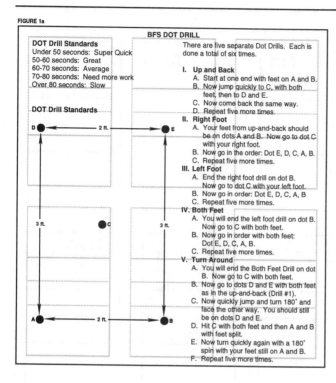

BFS DOT DRILL

DOT Drill Standards
Under 50 seconds: Super Quick
50-60 seconds: Great
60-70 seconds: Average
70-80 seconds: Need more work
Over 80 seconds: Slow

There are five separate Dot Drills. Each is done a total of six times.

I. Up and Back
A. Start at one end with feet on A and B.
B. Now jump quickly to C, with both feet, then to D and E.
C. Now come back the same way.
D. Repeat five more times.

II. Right Foot
A. Your feet from up-and-back should be on dots A and B. Now go to dot C with your right foot.
B. Now go in the order: Dot E, D, C, A, B.
C. Repeat five more times.

III. Left Foot
A. End the right foot drill on dot B. Now go to dot C with your left foot.
B. Now go in order: Dot E, D, C, A, B
C. Repeat five more times.

IV. Both Feet
A. You will end the left foot drill on dot B. Now go to C with both feet.
B. Now go in order with both feet: Dot E, D, C, A, B.
C. Repeat five more times.

V. Turn Around
A. You will end the Both Feet Drill on dot B. Now go to C with both feet.
B. Now go to dots D and E with both feet as in the up-and-back (Drill #1).
C. Now quickly jump and turn 180° and face the other way. You should still be on dots D and E.
D. Hit C with both feet and then A and B with feet split.
E. Now turn quickly again with a 180° spin with your feet still on A and B.
F. Repeat five more times.

FIGURE 2

PHYSICAL CONDITIONING & TESTING
Point Values

1. 440/400 Yard Run

20	Below 1:09
19	1:00-1:14
18	1:15-1:19
17	1:20-1:24
16	1:25-1:29
15	1:30-1:34
14	1:35-1:39
13	1:40-1:44
12	1:45-1:49
11	1:50-1:54
10	1:55-1:59
9	2:00-2:04
8	2:05-2:09
7	2:10-2:14
6	2:15-2:19
5	2:20-2:24
4	2:25-2:29
3	2:30-2:34
2	2:35-2:39
1	2:40-2:44
0	Above 2:45

2. Six Sidelines

10	Below 13.00
9	13.00-13.33
8	13.34-13.66
7	13.67-13.99
6	14.00-14.33
5	14.34-14.66
4	14.67-14.99
3	15.00-15.33
2	15.34-15.66
1	15.67-15.99
0	Above 16.00

3. 10 Foot Touches
Count each touch over the centerline and each over the 10' line. Touches = 30 points.
30 Seconds

4. 30 Foot Agility

10	Below 12.00
9	12.00-12.33
8	12.34-12.66
7	12.67-12.99
6	13.00-13.33
5	13.34-13.66
4	13.67-13.99
3	14.00-14.33
2	14.34-14.66
1	14.67-14.99
0	Above 15.00

5. Dot Drill

10	34-37
9	38-41
8	42-45
7	46-49
6	50-53
5	54-57
4	58-61
3	62-65
2	66-69
1	70-73
0	Below 74

6. Vertical Jump
Record the block jump, 2' takeoff and 1' takeoff. Inches = points.

FIGURE 3

SERVING Serve 10 balls to: Area 1, then Area 5, then Area 6. Use tape or cones to designate areas	**PASSING** Pass 10 balls from: Area 1, then Area 5, then Area 6. Coaches serve to ensure more validity. Use tape or cones for desired target areas.	**HITTING** Coaches toss 10 balls to: left side, then right side, then middle. partners count kills only, no tape shots or tips. Three hitters at a time.
SETTING Use setter training drills to evaluate.	**SUBJECTIVE EVALUATION** Narrow court doubles - tournament using different partners each round - keep individual points and record total.	**SUBJECTIVE EVALUATION** Six-on-six team play - use wash drills.

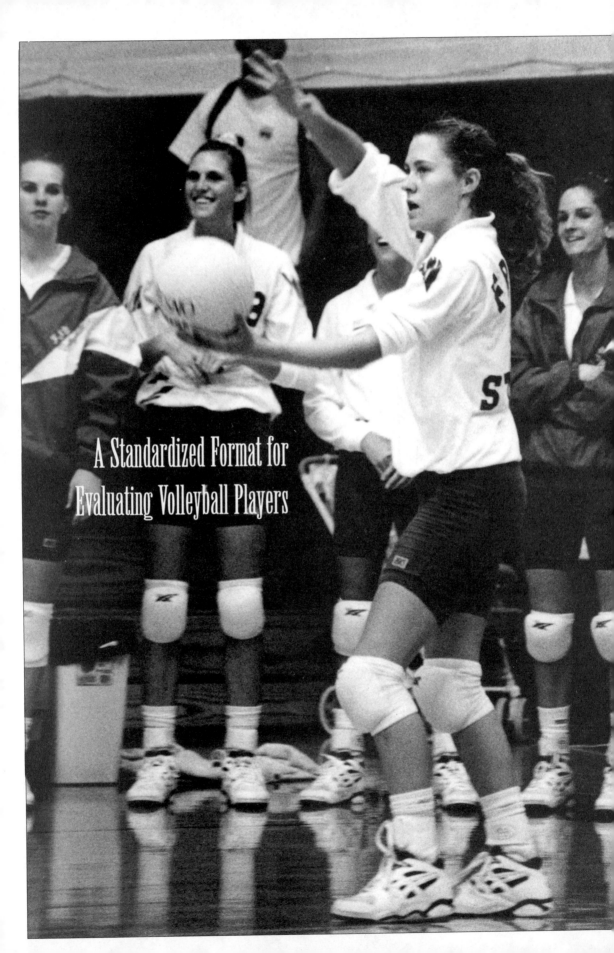

A Standardized Format for
Evaluating Volleyball Players

A Standardized Format for Evaluating Volleyball Players

Karen Guthmiller

During 1991, a standardized process of evaluation was implemented for the USA Volleyball Youth National Teams. The evaluation was two-fold: assessment of tournament play and assessment of performance during a tryout session. Specific directions were consistently administered to all personnel involved in the evaluation process. In other words, each evaluator was instructed to follow particular procedures when evaluating potential junior elite players during tournament play and tryout drills. Individuals assisting with the administration of drills during the tryout session also followed specific directions. The intent of this process was to be consistent in evaluating players from different geographic areas with various evaluators.

The guidelines for the evaluators to follow tournament play performance were definite. The rating scale was as follows: 1+,1,1- (superior); 2+, 2, 2- (excellent-good); 3+, 3, 3-(fair-poor). This same scale was utilized when evaluating performance during the tryout session. It was noted that these two components of evaluating were independent processes but the scores for each were comparable.

The tryout session was a standardized format including the following: directions, warm-up routine, position drills for setters, middle hitters and outside hitters and group drills of four vs. four or six vs. six. Guidelines for coaches assisting with administering drills were also implemented with standardized directions. The results of this procedure were positive. When considering all seven of the tryouts, the rating and ranking scores were consistent. This is an interesting point due to the fact that not all four junior elite coaches could be in attendance at every tryout site.

Photo: Univ. of Wisconsin

By using definite directions, applying specific rating scales to skills and techniques and implementing a precise structure of drills, an accurate assessment of talent can be made.

According to Hall and Rydberg (1995), in their article "Practice Variables that Enhance Skill Learning" (*Mental Training and Performance Enhancement*),

"Verbal feedback from the coach to the learner is the most important means of controlling the focus of learning. Feedback serves to direct the attention of the learner to a specific aspect of a skill. A learner has only so much attention to give to all aspects of a skill; once attention is directed in a specific area, the focus will be taken away from other areas."

APPLICATION

The implications of utilizing a standardized procedure for the junior elite program has practical applications. Numerous junior club programs and high school programs are faced with the dilemma of selecting teams. Even if one utilizes only the standardized format for a tryout session, the results can be beneficial. The drills used were designed for tryouts for the USA women's "B" team and U.S. Olympic Festival teams. This consistency can be expanded from the highest level of national team entrance evaluation to the beginning levels of player assessment. I encourage coaches to be consistent in evaluation procedures to enable us to "speak the same language" when talking about players and their abilities. Following are the standardized evaluations for the junior elite tryout.

JUNIOR ELITE TRYOUT - FOUR HOUR SESSION

1. Explain purpose of tryout and format structure.
2. Warm-up, stretch, partner pepper, count off to balance courts.
3. Left Side/Right Side Hitting Wave through in groups of five. Two coaches toss sets to left and right sides from same side of net. Example: Group 1 hits from left side. Group 2 hits from right side. Groups 3, 4, 5 shag and feed. Whistle every two minutes for

Considerations of Evaluation

■**Serve**
Type of serve used: floater/
topspin/jump/other
Can player serve to six positions?
Can player serve tough under
pressure?
Can player jump serve?

■**Attack**
Angle preferred to hit?
Can player hit line?
Can block bother player?
Can player hit play sets?

■**Blocking**
Position player's blocks: center/
outside
Can player penetrate over the net?
With hands? With elbows?
Note lateral mobility

■**Passing**
Can player consistently direct ball
to target area?
Note lateral mobility

■**Defense**
Ability to dig
Ability to react to tips
Recovery skills proficient?

■**Setting**
(only setters)
Consistency on delivery: 14 set/
85 set/51 set
Note set selection: isolates
blockers
Jump sets
Attacking ability

■**Attitude**
Competitiveness
Coachability
Reaction with teammates
Reaction to pressure situations
Emotional temperament

■**Physical/Athleticism**
Quickness/balance
Jump ability

wave. Rotate until all groups hit from both sides. Separate setters from other players.

4. Setter Progression - Setter release from right back (use large group: divide into setters, targets, feeders to rotate).
   a. Set: 14
      (1.) Coach toss
      (2.) Pass (use feeder group)
      (3.) Dig (use feeder group)
   b. Set: 85

5. Middle and Outside Groups of four.

6. a. Controlled offense and defense. One group offense; one group defense: one front court, three back court; extra groups shag. Coach tosses ball to passer who hits from outside (left side). Defense plays ball out. After offense hits five balls rotate groups. Wave team of four every three minutes.

7. b. Deep hit game-winner's side. No block, right front sets. Set ball behind 3-meter line. Coach initiates play with free ball to winner's side of court. Game to five points. Winner stays on winner's side only two consecutive times.

8. Break, evaluators meet, coaches measure vertical jump and reach.

9. Groups by positions: setters, outside, middle.

10. Four groups of four on each court (two groups of setters, two groups of hitters). Hit for 1-1/2 minutes, then switch.
    a. Coach tosses to setter, who sets to all hitters in one group. (Note: setters rotate among themselves, not with hitters.) Set 51s first, all others shag.
    b. Next group of hitters comes on to hit. Coach tosses balls to same setters who set 51s to new group.
    c. Switch setters who now set to first group of hitters. Set 51s.
    d. Now second group of hitters hits 51s from second group of setters.

11. Four vs. Six
    Setters rotate within their own system. Three hitters in a group as follows: one middle hitter, two outside hitters. Three minutes, then wave four on offense vs. six on defense. Setters release from right back on both sides. Team of four receives free ball, left front hitter passes it and setter can set any of three hitters. Defense plays it out. Switch setter to right front on side of six to repeat drill.

12. Break - drink, reshuffle teams if necessary.

13. Six vs. Six
    a. Setters rotate within their own system. One side receives five balls to side out. They then wave through, offense - defense - shaggers.
    b. Wash drill; setters rotate within their own system.
       (1.) One ball served for sideout.
       (2.) Serving team receives free ball.
       (3.) Play to five points.
       (4.) Rotate after scoring two "big points."
       (5.) Offense is 4-1-5.

   (6.) Defense is man back.
  c. Regular scoring game.
   (1.) Play to 11 points.
   (2.) Offense is 4-1-5.
   (3.) Defense is man back.
 14. Closing Remarks.

GUIDELINES FOR COACHES DIRECTING DRILLS
General Considerations
1. Keep directions short and concise.
2. Do not give instruction on skills, simply direct drills.
3. Criteria evaluators are considering:
 a. Setters
  (1.) Consistency in delivery.
  (2.) Decision making capabilities.
  (3.) Deception.
 b. Middle hitters
  (1.) Ability to dominate at the net offensively and defensively.
 c. Outside hitters
  (1.) Ability to terminate play.
  (2.) Passing and defensive skills.
4. Intent of drills
 a. Be consistent in tempo and rhythm.
 b. Be consistent in tossing or hitting balls.

A rating scale was defined to evaluate specific skills, athleticism and attitude. Each of these areas was further broken down for an evaluator to pay attention to specific considerations.

GUIDELINES FOR EVALUATORS
Purpose of Tryout
1. To identify potential elite players for the national team program.
2. To evaluate players in tournament play and in a formal tryout session.
3. To isolate a potential player when evaluating.
4. To collect information for national team.

NOTES FOR EVALUATION
1. Evaluate each player with form, observing tournament performance.
2. Evaluate again observing try-out performance.
3. Use the rating scale 1, 2, 3 with plus or minus.
4. Evaluate physical potential and technical skills.
5. Evaluate on tryout performance, not reputation.
6. Rank by position: setters, middles, outsides.
7. Draw line at elite level.
8. Rank top 12 players of tryout.
9. Setters, note in order of importance:
 a. Consistency in delivery;
 b. Decision making capabilities;
 c. Deception.
10. Middle hitters:
 a. Ability to dominate at the net offensively and defensively.

11. Outside hitters:

11. Outside hitters:
    a. Ability to terminate play;
    b. Passing and defensive skills.

Karen Guthmiller is the athletic director at Lee College in Baytown, Texas, and is a USA Volleyball CAP certified coach.

PLAYER EVALUATION
for Tournament Performance

FIGURE 1

No.	Name	Serve	Attack	Block	Passing	Defense	Setting	Attitude	Physical/ Athleticism

FIGURE 2   **Junior Elite Tryout**

Jersey No.	Name	Rating	Rating	Notes	Final Rating

Teaching Skills to New Players

JERRY GREGG

We would not get through the day if we did not make assumptions about a whole range of things, from the nature of being to what a burrito tastes like. Like you, I have made a number of assumptions about my coaching, about volleyball and about my players. These assumptions color everything I do. Some of the things I assume are simple and straightforward; some may need a little explanation; others may be wrong.

First, I assume that all my players want to play and to succeed, even those whose parents drag them in by their ankles. Second, these players never want to make a mistake. With that in mind, if a player does not function it is a result of one or two major factors:

According to Gregg, players most often wrestle with two issues: making mistakes and knowing what to do.

1) Players do not want to make mistakes and they do not want to look foolish. They do not want to disappoint their teammates, their parents or their coach. Have you ever had a player who, during a match, kept looking at you rather than the opponent? This is a player who is very concerned about making a mistake. And that is also a player who will likely make a mistake. As coaches we should spend more time convincing younger players that mistakes are merely information, not punishment. This is a hard lesson to teach and an even harder lesson to learn. Repetition is the watchword.

2) The other reason why players do not function is that they simply do not know what to do. The solution here is obvious: help them learn what to do and put them into practice situations where they can do it.

It is these two issues, making mistakes and knowing what to do, which players wrestle with most often. Remember, a player who makes a mistake, particularly in a contest, has already been punished. It is at this moment they learn something from the experience.

With regard to knowing what to do, coaches need to define and provide examples of end or goal behaviors for their players. Ample opportunity for players to develop their skills on their own must be built into the learning process. Even at the highest levels of play, the coach should make players aware of what they are doing, providing constant encouragement and suggestions. It has been my experience that if players know what they are doing and have the opportunity to do it, the differences between where they are and where you want them to be will begin to draw closer. Again, patience, encouragement and trust in the process are what a coach must learn to live by.

> Remember, a player who makes a mistake, particularly in a contest, has already been punished. It is at this moment they learn something from the experience.

BASIC REQUIREMENTS

Each time I define basic requirements for success in volleyball, examples emerge to prove me wrong. Case in point: slow players and small players. Both have been successful, although it is not easy for a player who is both small and slow to be successful. However, I would say that successful play requires at least average athletic ability with the ability to jump being a key factor. But, do not limit yourself. I have good players on my team who seem glued to the floor. Be flexible.

20

A player needs to know what to do . A coach's responsibility is to provide the proper example of how the skill is to be executed.

Weiss and Wiese (1989) assert that a "number of studies have revealed that athletes share common motivational themes for participating in sport. These themes are competence, fitness, fun, team atmosphere and affiliation.

Competence motives include achieving personal goals, learning and improving skills, liking the challenges inherent in sport, wanting to be competent and and wanting to win.

Fitness motives include getting and staying in shape, becoming stronger and being physically active.

Fun has always rated highly as a participation motive, no matter the athlete's age or intensity. It is often lost in working on skills and strategies. However, if fun is not incorporated into practices, athletes will lose their motivation.

Team atmosphere includes players' liking teamwork and team spirit, enjoying being on a team and feeling part of a group. Although much remains to be learned about the importance of team cohesion, athletes say that this is a prime reason for their continuing to participate.

Affiliation includes liking to be with friends and wanting to make new friends. Both the affiliation and the team atmosphere themes reflect the importance of the social dimension of sport participation.

(Weiss, Ph.D., Maureen R. and Diane M. Wiese. Motivating your volleyball players. *Coaching Volleyball*, December/January 1989, 6-10.)

The question of desire always seems to arise when discussing requirements for successful play. I am not really sure what desire is in regard to sports, or how I identify that quality in a 13-year-old. Whatever it is, I suspect that it is overrated. Should kids be "fired up?" Is that desire? I seem to spend more time calming kids down and getting them focused than getting them excited. I contend that if a player is human and entering a match, they are excited. Is desire something you can see? There are lots of "foaming at the mouth" type players who cannot pass a lick and many good passers who look bored.

If a player appears unmotivated, it could mean that they do not see well, or they just do not know what to do. This player may have been hurt by a teammate's remark or by something the coach said or they fear making a mistake. At any rate, their performance level is low.

In contrast, the veteran or "go to" player may simply be someone who can track a ball through the air or who knows what to do in a given situation. This player may also be the one who knows that the coach or Mom and Dad will still love her if she fails and, therefore, is willing to take a risk.

Therefore, all we can really determine is whether or not a player or team is performing (e.g. did or did they not pass the ball?). Once again, motivating athletes to play volleyball is seldom an issue. What sport is more motivating than volleyball? I do not know of a game that is more fun to practice or play.

TECHNICAL

There are dozens of ways to execute every skill in volleyball and hundreds of adherents for each. In short, I have not found the answer, although I do recommend keeping things as simple as possible.

If you are unsure how to teach someone to pass, buy a book or a videotape. There are some good ones on the market. As someone who never played volleyball, I had to do a lot of looking, asking and reading in order to learn what little I do know. Take advantage of all available resources.

TEACHING

A player needs to know what to do. A coach's responsibility is to provide the proper example of how the skill is to be executed. A young and eager coach can demonstrate the skill, but after years of various sports, some of us have body parts that hurt. I now "simulate" rather than demonstrate. I have made some use of video in providing the proper example and often use older players with good skills as demonstrators.

Another critical teaching component is the effect of negative and/or positive reinforcement. Some coaches appear to be very tough on athletes, who, in turn, play well and emerge from the experience apparently unscathed. Perhaps these players understand that the criticism is directed at their behavior rather than their character.

My style is different. I do not yell at my players any more than other coaches who say they do not yell at their players. I avoid such displays because it does not seem to achieve any desirable result. More than that,

I cannot take looking at sad, hurt or angry faces. I still rant and rave, but this emotion is not directed at someone. In most cases, I am trying to keep the mistake that a player just made from being the reason why they make the next one.

Philosophically, I believe that if a coach can "hook" a player in terms of their relationship with the athlete, you can push them a little harder. Most young players do not realize what they can do and often need a nudge to perform at a higher level. Still, those same players need to know that you believe they can perform at a higher level and that your occasional "foul tempers" are only intended as constructive criticism.

It is also the coach's responsibility to provide players proper feedback. Feedback can be provided in many ways, but most often it is verbal. Use key words, not speeches. Because egos are easily damaged in the early stages of skill acquisition, it might be best to preface and end your remarks to players with a compliment.

A special role for a coach is recognizing distinct capabilities and limitations a player might have in mastering a skill. Everyone is made differently, so no two people perform a skill identically. For example, Player X may not be able to straighten his arms fully. Player X still must pass a volleyball. How do I help Player X adapt to this special physical challenge? Thus, helping a player adapt what they can do to what needs to be done, whether you are talking about individual skills or playing systems, may just be what separates good coaches from the rest of the field.

Clearly, a coach needs to provide opportunity for players to develop skills. Thus, practice sessions were invented. Players need time to experiment in order to gain command of skills. If a player has a clear idea as to what to do, and if she can get good information as to what she is doing, then little more is needed than encouragement and the opportunity to work. Players will make the necessary changes themselves - you can count on it!

> Weiss and Wiese (1989) believe that coaches must provide appropriate instructional feedback.
> "What coaches say and how they say it are important aspects of motivating athletes. coaches should give immediate feedback about performance technique and strategy and make sure their messages are understood. A coach might observe an athlete's execution several times before providing instruction or understanding how to convey the information most effectively."

> Helping a player adapt what they can do to what needs to be done, whether you are talking about individual skills or playing systems, may just be what separates good coaches from the rest of the field.

When I began coaching volleyball after coaching football, I was struck by how little volleyball coaches talk during practice. As a football coach, I found myself talking all the time. My idea, I suppose, was that if you throw enough mud at the a fence, some of it is bound to stick. In contrast, the volleyball coaches I observed approached practice in a different way, defining the desired behaviors at the outset, observing the players and then providing feedback. I believe this player-centered approach is appropriate to teaching volleyball skills, an aspect of coaching I am continually working on.

During practice, coaches need to make drills appropriate to the skill. I once observed a two-hour setter's practice where players executed agility drills for 45 minutes. There may have been some Zen benefit in the situation that I did not recognize, but handling a volleyball, in my opinion, might have been more appropriate.

According to Chuck Erbe (1995), "As volleyball coaches, we need to understand what it takes to train a setter. What does it take to train a middle blocker or outside hitter? What does it take to train all aspects of the game? If the setter is the single most important person on the floor, we as coaches had better invest in that individual more time than any other person. We also give that person more repetitions and more guidance. In other words, if we want a specific set, we have to talk to them in terms of the height, the distance, the tempo and the end location. If we have not worked with them to give them information, then they do not know what is expected of them. If we have not given them thousands of repetitions to acquire the motor and muscle memory skills to enable them to have consistency and then train the movement skills to allow them to problem solve different setting situations, none of us as coaches can expect our setters to be consistent."

(Erbe, Chuck and Dan McDonough. Setter injury profiles and preventive strategies. *Critical Thinking on Setter Development*, March 1995, 70.)

Since the acquisition of volleyball skills often involves the laying down of new neural pathways, repetition is a must. I use very few drills, perhaps three variable drills for each skill, and do them over and over. Almost any drill can be dressed up a bit to prevent boredom. Give players a quarter if they can pass to some small target, but have them pass again and again.

I am not as sold on progressive drills as I once was. I am more inclined to get right at it when it comes to skill development without a lot of interim drills. I still use progressive drills (progressing from simpler to more complex problems), but I am beginning to question the value of the drill "in the middle."

Do not be afraid to use individual drills where the player performs alone, but always, in the same practice, use drills where players are forced to execute skills in conjunction with at least one other player. In multiple player drills, players must communicate verbally and through movement begin to deal with distractions. Repeat these drills often.

How much time should be devoted to conditioning when working with young players? Frankly, only teams that are technically sound play long enough for conditioning to be a factor. Do you want a well-conditioned team that cannot perform the skills required or a team that is successful, but a little tried? I will error on the side of the latter. Drills can be designed to accomplish both conditioning and skill development, but when working with young players, lean toward skill development. The value of tough physical drills for young players seems to lie primarily in the fact that they go home thinking that they worked hard.

Above all, be patient. You will see errors repeated. Keep spelling out what should happen and what is happening, and keep providing encouragement. John Kessel, USA Volleyball director of program development and services, has a great idea when he asks his players to identify what they did right or wrong. Nothing is better in helping a player learn what should be done and where he is in regard to a skill. Through it all, keep telling players how great they are even if you have to bite your lip to do it. Then one day, your players will begin to hit and it will be because they are getting good sets and that will be because the pass to the setter is on target. Your team will be moving communication and they will be absolutely absorbed in the game. Soon you will wonder, "Who are these kids?!"

Rest assured, they will be your kids.

A balance needs to be struck between rote and game-like activities. Game-like drills force players to perform skills in an increasingly broad range of situations. Do both. Just remember, in order to pass well, a young player needs to pass a lot.

Photo: University of Hawai'i

SECONDARY FACTORS

The following factors will make

teaching skills to a 13 year-old much easier. Some are obvious and some require a bit of a stretch to accept. The reader can accept or reject at will. There is no order of importance:

1) Play as many multi-day tournaments as possible early in your season.

2) Keep an eye out for the relationships that are developing on your team. If players like one another, they are more supportive when mistakes are made and more rewarding of success.

3) Feed them. Darned if I know why, but if you cancel a practice and buy a team pizza, they will play better. That does not mean they chip in money. Quite the contrary; it means that you dig into your own pocket and be sure they know that you did so. It is, and continues to be, my secret weapon.

CONCLUSION

Volleyball coaches sometimes play things a bit close to the chest in regards to sharing information, whereas football coaches will spill their guts for a beer. If something in this article helps, great. If you see something you disagree with, let me and everyone else know. Above all, it is most important to share what you know.

Jerry Gregg is the head girls' volleyball coach at Cypress High School in Cypress, Calif., and is a USA Volleyball CAP certified coach.

Section II: The Serve

Short Zone Serving

Short Zone Serving

Short zone serving is an area that a lot of coaches shy away from, mostly because they feel it is too easy of a serve or it is not effective enough for what they want to accomplish during a match. In fact, many coaches believe that they should simply let their players stand back and just "let it rip" because that serve might be a lot more effective. In reality, coaches can use the short zone serve, primarily to try to catch a receiving team off guard if the receivers are out of position.

Catching a team out of position is obviously a good way to use the short zone serve. One way that a number of coaches do not think to use a short serve, especially if you are playing a better team that receives the ball really well, is using it to disrupt their offense. If a team has a big player and that player subs out in the front row, the coach is subbing that player out for a good reason—probably because they cannot pass the ball or play defense quite as well. Perhaps their ball control skills are not as good. If the coach has that player in the front row to attack, there is nothing that says you cannot serve to them while they are there.

Even though a short zone serve will more than likely not result in an ace, it does serve to catch a team out of position.

Being able to hit your zone and have a good, consistent short zone serve and put it right in this player's lap is a good way to take them out of their offense because 1) it forces that person to receive; and 2) when they are receiving, they may be taking their mind off attacking. Also, if you have a receiver who is receiving deep in the court in a three-person reception pattern, having them move up close to the net to receive can also disrupt their offense from the standpoint that it affects their attack approach, angles, etc. The last thing it can really affect is the amount of time that the setter has to think about the choices on the set. When the pass is traveling from 20-25 feet up to the net, there is a lot of air time and the setter can get there a little quicker, think about what is going on and maybe make a more educated decision about where to set. If the pass is at the attack line and the setter only has 8-10 feet worth of air time on the ball to think about what is going on, reaction time is limited; the setter does not have as much time to think about where to set and it may ultimately affect choices.

The down side about short zone serving in general is it gives the receiving team less time to react, but also gives your defense or your blockers less time to react. The blockers have to be aware that the ball is going to be passed to the setter rather quickly and they are going to have less time to see the approach patterns. Also, if the team that is receiving has a front-row setter, the ball is getting to that potential attacker a lot quicker; your defense is going to have less time to get into position.

If you are having one of your servers execute a short zone serve, I would recommend not having them play left back defense, simply because they may not have time to serve and travel all the way to the left back position if there is a front-row setter. The setter can jump to that position a lot quicker. You may want to adjust your defensive base position in that way.

TYPES OF SERVES

The three types of short zone serves are:

According to Pingel, there are three types of short zone serves: the high arc serve, the flat serve and the intermediate depth serve.

1) **The High Arc Serve**: This is a really effective serve. A lot of teams, men's in particular, are using this serve. A team is not going to get a considerable number of aces off of it, but you have a lower chance of error and it is easier to hit your targets.

Technically speaking, with the high arc serve, you still want the ball to cross the net somewhere between the top of the antenna and the top of the net. It is not going to be so high that it is going all the way back, 15-20 feet.

Ideally, you want to have this serve land from the attack line and up. In order to get that, you want to serve the ball nice and high so that when it is crossing the net, it is definitely on its way down. The big technical difference on this is that instead of the normal toss out in front of the server like you are going to serve in the deep zone, you want to toss the ball slightly back so that you are contacting the bottom of the ball, not the back of the ball. There is a lot of travel time involved with this serve—plenty of time for a person in the back row to scoot up. Again, you are not looking for aces with this serve; you are looking to take the receiving team out of the reception pattern.

If you have a short zone serve to middle front, you may have three or four players converging on the ball and it clogs everything up into the middle. If you are playing against a team that runs a swing offense and your outside hitter is having to come in and receive that ball, it could really affect it. Some squads that have the receiving teams very deep almost beg you to short zone serve because it quickens their offense even more. Knowing that, you may not want to short zone serve.

With the short zone serve, you have a little less chance of error because if you miss, you definitely want to miss deep. You do not want to miss short because it goes in the net. If it travels a little bit deeper, that is alright, too. The down side is that you are not going to get many aces and it is an easier ball to pass to target than the quicker serve.

Some teams that have the receiving teams very deep almost beg you to short zone serve because it quickens their offense even more. Knowing that, you may not want to short zone serve.

2) **The Flat Serve**: The next serve is a flatter ball. It does not travel nearly as high. It is basically the same type of toss that you would use for a deep zone serve; however, you hit it much more lightly. The idea is that it is barely going to clear the top of the net and it is going to drop off once it gets past the net.

The advantage of this serve is that it does get to the receiving team a lot quicker and it has a better chance of catching them off guard, especially if they are receiving deep. However, because it is moving a little bit quicker and flatter, it is a harder ball to receive and pass right to the target. When you are receiving a ball in the back row, you want to pass it to target, but you have a little bit of room for error in depth; you have a 20-foot pass and you can adjust to the speed a little bit. Also, you have a little bit longer time to see the ball. On a short zone serve that is really flat and gets on you in a hurry, you almost have to dig it and take some of the speed off of it. Otherwise, you are looking at an over-pass. Again, with this flat serve, the toss is out in front. If you hit it too strongly, it goes right back into the heart of the reception. As a result, there is room for error.

From a technical standpoint, the toss stays out in front; you are hitting it left and trying to get it close to the top of the net. However, your chance for error is obviously a lot higher. You have a flat serve that can clip the top of the net, or if you hit it too hard, it is going to carry out. You should not have a problem with serving it too deep. Plus, there is added room for error on contact. For example, if you hit it a little bit high on the hand instead of down where you should normally be serving, you could fluff it a little bit. Or, if you hit off-center, it is not going to have enough speed on it to reach all the way to the net.

On all short zone serves, the 2 zone is probably one of the most difficult because the ball has to travel a little bit longer; plus, you have the sideline to contend with. In addition, you are going cross-court, which is adding to the distance. But, if you have a server who is really good at zone 2 serving, it can probably be the most effective serve in your repertoire, especially if the setter is coming out of that position. If the setter is releasing out of right back, serving to that position always works well. The most important thing is that the distance from a right front passer to the setting position is reduced. If the setter is facing where the pass is coming from and the serve goes to the attack line or sideline, the setter, for the most part, is going to have his or her back to the middle attacker and the outside attacker. The setter is not going to be able to use peripheral vision to see if the middle is coming in on time, etc.

Even if it is a high, arcing serve to zone 2, the receiver has small room for error and the setter is going to be taken out of the reception or out of the flow of the offense at that point.

A serve over to zone 4 is pretty — and advantageous — because you are going to bring your receiver up and reduce the approach distance; however from a setter's standpoint, it is just like receiving the ball from the back row. The distance is just about the same and they still get to see their middle attacker coming in.

3) **Intermediate Depth Serve**: The third short zone serve is a combination of both of these serves. It is a serve where you are looking for more aces but you are also looking to disrupt the reception pattern. It is an intermediate serve.

With this serve, the ball is not going to land very close to the net, but you do want to have your front-row receivers receive the ball. You would utilize this serve if a receiving team would be using a service reception W or a "U" or an offense where there is a person playing short. The idea is that you would be serving right at the short zone receiver's shoulder, head, etc. If they are going to receive the ball, they have to take the ball very high, move back and adjust. If the front-row people are going to step in, it is going to be a situation where they actually have to move fairly quickly behind the ball and they have to play a ball in front. What it is

"I think a team that has a serving game that fits its style of play also wins. Take a look at some of the ways to evaluate serving. In ace-to-error ratio, how many mistakes are you willing to give up to score points by the ace? The ace is the easiest way to score. One contact of the ball and you have a point. As we all know, to get aces, you have to up the tempo and press down on the accelerator. You have to get the ball over in a tough fashion to create the ace. When you do that, you also create increased errors. How many are you willing to give up in search of an ace? I think it is different at different levels of play."

(Mike Hebert. Ten reasons why teams win. *Coaching Volleyball*, April/May 1995.)

supposed to do is create some confusion. If you have a receiving team that does not communicate very well, the front-row person may take a step for the ball because they think that they have to receive it and the back-row people see that step and stop. It should create some communication problems. This should be a fairly quick ball that barely clears the top of the net. In instructing your players, tell them to aim for a particular short zone receiver's shoulders or head. If you have a zone receiver who is used to receiving the ball, he/she might not be able to get out of the way and it will clog up some things.

The advantage of this serve is that you have a decreased chance of error. If you hit the serve a little too hard, it is going to continue back to the back-row receivers and you are going to say, "Well, it was not quite as an effective serve as we wanted." But, you are not going to have an inordinate number of errors. Again, if it is served correctly and you hit your targets, it can be very effective in disrupting reception; because of the speed, you may get a few aces off of it, also.

The down side to this serve is that it requires a highly accurate serve to be effective. If you do not have an accurate serve and it goes right at the player's shoulders or head, it becomes just another serve, like a down ball or a free ball that would go right into the heart of the reception.

As for technique, the intermediate serve is much like the flat serve. The toss is out in front and you hit the back of the ball instead of the bottom.

SERVING STRATEGIES

From a strategic standpoint, depending on what level you are playing or what kind of team you have, you must adjust your serving patterns. If you are playing a team that is a very strong receiving team, you may not get a large number of aces off of a short zone serve; by the same token, you are not going to get a whole lot of aces off of a deep zone serve, either. As a coach, you have to decide what is going to be the most effective way for your serving team to have an advantage in serving. Perhaps it is just a matter of disrupting the offense and bringing all of the players together. It is something that is a change of pace and teams may not be used to seeing it if they do not do it themselves. If your team serves a lot of short zone serves, that means you are going to be serving a lot of them in practice and your reception patterns will be used to reacting to the short zone serves. It is something that can help both your receiving and your serving.

Whether you call your zones from the bench or you talk about what your serving strategies are going to be at the beginning of the game, coaches should always take time to discuss it. A lot of times, we as coaches fall into the trap of talking so much about offense and defense that we do not talk about strategies before the game or at time-outs. If you are a coach who calls the zones from the bench, then all the servers have to do is worry about going back and looking for the number. Make sure you discuss serving, as well as what attacks have been going well or what

According to John Dunning, "Each team must develop its own serving style and philosophy. There are many serves to choose from: the overhead floater, the roundhouse floater, the standing topspin, the jump spin serve, the sky serve, the deep serve, the sidespin serve, etc. Each team should have at least a few different types of serves.

Strategy:
1. Serve the toughest possible serve.
2. Serve the poorest passer.
3. Serve the most likely attacker.
4. Serve to interrupt the offense.
5. Serve short and long.
6. Serve a substitute.

(John Dunning. Serve to win. *Coaching Volleyball*, March 1994.)

adjustments need to be made on defense.

The biggest fear from a server's standpoint is the fear of making an error on the short zone serve. Obviously, from a confidence standpoint, the problem has to be taken care of in practice. Try to put your players into gamelike situations as much as possible in practice situations where if you are a coach who calls the zones from the bench, you are doing that in practice. It does not do any good for you to tell them to serve wherever they want to or go with their own mix and then you jump into a game and all of a sudden they have to adjust and look over to the sidelines for the serving zones.

Of course, you do not necessarily have to call the zones; if there are two people back in the serving line, have the other person tell the server what zone to serve or have the server simply turn to their partner and give them the zone that they are going for. Try to have them even out the serves, using both the deep zone and short zone. A lot of times, if you just let your players go back and serve wherever they want to go, it is going to be 75% deep zones and then you have to remind them of the short zone serves, also.

SUMMARY

Short zone serving can be effective. In fact, do not be afraid to utilize the tactic when you get into a rally score game. I am sure every coach has thought about what the strategies are in utilizing short zone serves; in effect, you have to do the same thing in the rally score games that got you there in the first place. If it is attacking, blocking or defense, you cannot worry. It is the same thing with short zone serving. If it was effective in the first four games, it should still be effective—if not more—in the fifth game.

Tom Pingel is the head girls' volleyball coach for the Circle City Volleyball Club in Indianapolis, Ind.

"The goal of all practice is to improve performance levels, especially in stressful situations. To do this, we must learn how to repel stress and learn to challenge the limits of our ability to focus."

(John Dunning. Serve to win. *Coaching Volleyball*, March 1994.)

The Short Serve:
An Underutilized Tactic

The Short Zone Serve: An Underutilized Tactic

Bernie Goldfine

Most tactical considerations concerning serving are dependent upon the ability of volleyball players to serve to the six universally recognized zones of an opponent's court. Serving to the deep zones (1, 6 and 5) rather than the short zones (2, 3 and 4) allows players to use more power, thereby producing relatively higher velocity, lower trajectory serves. Despite the common misconception that tough serves are only those hit deep with high velocity and/or lots of movement, strategically placed, low-velocity short serves can be equally tough for opponents to receive. However, many high school and college teams either seldom or never use the serve to the short zones (2, 3, and 4) in competition. In fact, a study of selected men's and women's collegiate teams found that only approximately two percent of serves were played in the area between the attack line and net (Byl, 1989). The tendency of teams not to use short serves deprives them of an excellent opportunity to wreak havoc upon opponents.

According to Goldfine, players must be able to serve successfully to the six universally recognized zones of an opponent's court.

The objectives of this article are to present: (a) tactical reasons for using the short serve; (b) elements of and guidelines for effective short serving; (c) considerations for practicing the short serve; and (d) factors to consider for incorporating short serve strategies.

TACTICAL REASONS FOR USING THE SHORT SERVE

Coaches vary on their philosophies of serving: some have a conservative approach to serving and direct their players simply to keep the ball in play; others see the serve as an opportunity to score points or exert pressure on the opponent's serve-reception. Coaches must assess their team's athletic abilities and skill development level, relative to their competition, to determine an appropriate serving strategy. For example, if a team does not match up to its opponents at the net and, consequently, has trouble scoring, a coach may call for the players to serve aggressively. Part of an aggressive serving strategy entails short serves, which can produce aces, force poor passes or disrupt the opponent's offensive patterns.

> Coaches vary on their philosophies of serving: some have a conservative approach to serving and direct their players simply to keep the ball in play; others see the serve as an opportunity to score points or exert pressure on the opponent's serve-reception. Coaches must assess their team's athletic abilities and skill development level, relative to their competition, to determine an appropriate serving strategy.

The most desirable result of a short serve is an ace. This usually occurs when opponents are caught completely off-guard. However, judging the effectiveness of this tactic exclusively by the number of aces recorded is not a valid assessment; several other results can be achieved, as with any accurately placed serve.

First, short serving commonly causes opponents to pass balls over the net for easy kill opportunities. These over-passes usually occur because the passers, positioned deep in the court, do not anticipate the short serve. Consequently, they are late reacting and moving to the serve, which results in poor body positioning, flawed technique and poor ball control.

Second, the ability to serve accurately to the short zones rather than exclusively to the deep zones is essential to the most basic serving strategy: forcing a particular player to pass the ball. That player may be the opposition's

ZONE CHART

4	3	2
5	6	1

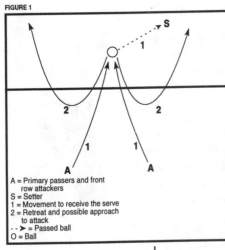

FIGURE 1

A = Primary passers and front
    row attackers
S = Setter
1 = Movement to receive the serve
2 = Retreat and possible approach
    to attack
- - ➤ = Passed ball
O = Ball

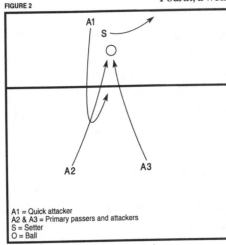

FIGURE 2

A1 = Quick attacker
A2 & A3 = Primary passers and attackers
S = Setter
O = Ball

worst passer; a substitute who may not be adequately warmed up or mentally prepared; a player who has just committed an error; or a key player whom you hope to fatigue or frustrate with a barrage of serves (Selinger, 1986).

Third, short serving may effectively force a team out of its offense by producing a pass which (a) the setter cannot reach and another player must set or (b) the setter can set, but is unable to run the middle or other quick options or combinations. In this era of passing specialization, with many teams choosing to receive serve with two, three or four passers, such patterns leave areas of the court unprotected. Often those areas are the short serve zones, especially zone 3. If one or both of the primary passers are front-row attackers (as in the swing attack), the short serve can force them to alter their approach and attack patterns. Moreover, if these primary attackers have to pass near the net, retreat and then approach, their athleticism and stamina can be tested repeatedly. Executing these pre-attack maneuvers effectively is extremely difficult (Figure 1) and can pressure the opponent's offensive capabilities.

Fourth, a well-placed short serve can also produce traffic among the opposition along the net as the setter attempts to penetrate and hitters try to position themselves for approaches. If attackers are deliberately positioned close to the net, out of the serve reception pattern, the short serve can lead to confusion as the attackers retreat toward the attack line and the passers move forward to pass the ball (Figure 2). This convergence on the same area of the court can inhibit the decision-making and movement of both passers and attackers.

Finally, setters penetrating from the back row often have difficulty seeing balls served to zone 2, since they generally try to position themselves toward the strong side of the court, facing the zone 4. A serve to this area makes it difficult for the setter to track the ball and be in sync with the hitters. Also, a serve to the 4 zone does not afford a setter penetrating from the left back a good look at the served ball, thus diminishing the chances to organize an effective attack.

ELEMENTS OF AND GUIDELINES FOR EFFECTIVE SHORT SERVING

Considering all of the tactical reasons to integrate a short serving strategy into a team's gameplan, why don't more teams do so? As previously mentioned, some coaches prefer – or their players' talents may dictate – a more conservative serving strategy. Another major deterrent is that mastering a highly effective short serve is difficult. An inability to achieve the desired results of short serving can frustrate and discourage both players and coaches to the point of abandonment or under-utilization of this tactic.

The two key elements to effective short serving are accurate placement and deceptive serving motion. Unlike serves to the deep zones, which can be effective even if they land within 10 feet of the end line, the short serve leaves much less margin for error. Short serves that land a few feet behind the 3-meter line generally are easily passed by the opponent (with the exception of a well-struck, unpredictable floater); whereas, those that are contacted with insufficient power and loft may end up in the net. Such precision placement of the short serve forces receivers to move the maximum distance forward, often resulting in receiving errors.

The effectiveness of a short serve is also a function of the deceptiveness of the server's motion. As Hsiung (1990) points out in his article, *Baseball and The Volleyball Serve*, "The hard serves to deep zones 1, 5 and 6 (volleyball's fastballs) set up our change-ups or short serves to zones 2, 3 and 4." Just as baseball pitchers do not want to give any indication that they are changing up speeds, to be truly deceptive, volleyball players need to use body motion patterns for the short serve similar to those they would use when serving deep, hard serves, letting up on their swing only at the last second. Players need to be aware of when they are obviously giving away their intentions to short serve (e.g., through an exaggerated tilt upward of the non-hitting shoulder, significantly altered arm swing or positioning behind the end line). If a short serve is well-disguised, the opponent's ability to react is impaired.

Photo: Christopher Broadhurst

According to Goldfine, "the effectiveness of a short serve is a function of the deceptiveness of the server's motion."

CONSIDERATIONS FOR PRACTICING THE SHORT SERVE

"Serving is a volleyball skill that all coaches feel is important, but it often gets scant attention in practice" (MacGregor, 1988). Quantity and quality of practice time allotted to the short serve during workouts obviously has a bearing on players' serving abilities and repertoire. Serving consistently and effectively to the short zones requires a regular practice regimen.

Because serving is the only volleyball skill that does not require reactions to a ball in play (i.e., the player initiates this action rather than reacting to a pass, dig, set, spike or block), players can practice on their own time serving at the short zones with a basket of balls. Even as little as five or 10 minutes of practice a day will enhance development of this skill.

Serving is a volleyball skill that all coaches feel is important, but it often gets scant attention in practice.

Concerning team practice, serving practice should be held at the beginning, middle and end of practice sessions to simulate game conditions when players are fresh, tired or exhausted (Scates, 1984). Targets such as chairs, mats or cones can be placed between the attack line and net. Having coaches seated in chairs as short serve targets can make this type of target serving more enticing and fun.

As players become more consistent at hitting the short zones, competitive drills can be added to the workout to enhance concentration and add an element of pressure similar to what they will face during match play. For example, the team could be divided into two squads, with the winning side determined by the first squad (1) to hit a certain number of short serves within the attack line or (2) to hit targets set up within the short zones. Once players have mastered serving to the short zones in a deceptive fashion, they should practice a variety of serves against various serve reception formations in drill and scrimmage situations to experience "real match" conditions. Serving short serves in wash or scrimmage situations should build a player's confidence to execute in real matches. Finally, in scrimmage situations, players should periodically be challenged to identify the vulnerable short areas, without direction from the coach. Allowing players to make these decisions can foster a confident and aggressive attitude toward short serving.

FACTORS TO CONSIDER FOR INCORPORATING SHORT SERVE STRATEGIES

Not every player will be a good candidate to serve the short zones. Those who exclusively rely on hard top spin or jump serves generally have trouble serving these areas. Therefore, rather than expending a great deal of time and effort trying to teach these top spin servers how to serve the short zones, improvement of their power serves should be stressed. The off-season is a good time for these players to develop their short serving skills. It should also be noted that relative to team serving strategy, these top spin and jump servers complement the players who can serve deep and short floaters, thereby making it difficult for the opposition's passers to anticipate velocity, location and movement of serves.

Not every player will be a good candidate to serve the short zones. Those who exclusively rely on hard top spin or jump serves generally have trouble serving these areas.

A good strategy for incorporating the short serve is to alternate short and deep serves to the opponent's poor passers, thus forcing them to move up and then back constantly. Another effective pattern is to serve short continually to the same zone until a team proves it can effectively pass and run its offense. Finally, serving to short zones on an intermittent, non-patterned basis is the best strategy of yielding aces and poor passes.

To employ short serving tactics effectively, coaches must emphasize this skill to their players. Development should start in the off-season or the beginning of the competitive season. Practice time should be allocated regularly, specifically for this tactic. During the first part of the competitive season, coaches should help build a player's confidence by calling for short serves, even if that individual has missed on previous attempts. The ability of a majority of a team's players to serve short effectively can be a valuable tool in assisting a team on its quest for success.

References
Byl, J. (1989). Two-person service reception. *Coaching Volleyball*, October/November, 15-17.
Hsiung, S. (1990). Baseball and the volleyball serve. *Coaching Volleyball*, October/November, 16-17.
MacGregor, L. (1988). SBR, A winning acronym. *Coaching Volleyball*, October/November, 18-21.
Scates, A.E. (1984). *Winning Volleyball*. Newton, MA: Allyn and Bacon, Inc.
Selinger, A. (1986). *Arie Selinger's Power Volleyball*. New York: St. Martin's Press.

Bernie Goldfine, Ph.D., is an associate professor in the Department of Health, Physical Education and Recreation at Kennesaw State College in Marietta, Ga.

This Serve Is For You

This Serve Is For You

STEPHANIE SCHLEUDER AND
DOROTHY FRANCO-REED

Imagine this....it is the fifth game of the match and your team is behind, 12-14. Your team gets a sideout, but before you finish your sigh of relief, you realize that your most erratic server, Suzie Choke, is coming back to serve. Suzie looks nervously to the bench, waiting for direction. It is your call — should she play it safe or go for it with her jump serve? Although Suzie's jump serves are in-court three out of four times, flashing through our minds are memories of the ones that have sailed out-of-bounds into the bleachers. Throwing caution to the wind, you signal her to go for it! You close your eyes and pray as Suzie steps back to serve. Miraculously, she jump serves four consecutive aces to win the match. In the post-match interviews you calmly describe to the reporters your complete confidence that Choke would come through in the clutch.

According to the authors, although the jump serve was initially seen in the early 1960s, the technique existed in relative obscurity until the 1984 Olympics.

BACKGROUND

Although the jump serve was initially seen in the early 1960s, the technique existed in relative obscurity until the 1984 Olympics. During the Los Angeles Games, the Brazilian men's team reacquainted the volleyball world with this skill. Since that time, the jump serve has been recognized as an exciting skill and it is being introduced at all levels of the game.

DETERMINE YOUR SERVING PHILOSOPHY

Each coach must determine his/her own philosophy on putting the ball in play: Do you want your players to serve for points or do you want to put the ball safely in play? If you elect to have players serve for points you will obviously risk more missed serves, but you will also place more pressure on your opponent's ability to pass the ball. Electing to serve less aggressively increases the importance of your team's ability to block or dig an opponent's attack and then rely on your transition offense to score points. The decision should be based upon your team's individual and collective talents in these areas. There is no doubt that the jump serve is an advanced, high-risk technique. But the payoff for accepting the risk can be seen in a combination of positive results:

• The serve becomes an offensive weapon.

• The serve encourages and enhances an aggressive style of play from your team, both physically and mentally.

• Your opponents are forced to prepare for an additional tactical and technical aspect of your team's play.

STATISTICAL CONSIDERATIONS

You should continually evaluate your players' progress and performance. Once your players demonstrate proficiency in the jump serve during practice and scrimmages, it is time to try the skill in actual competition. Jim Coleman, director of the U.S. National Teams Training Center, was helpful in outlining statistical guidelines for evaluating the effectiveness of the jump serve. The following areas should be considered:

Photo: Angelo State

Each coach must determine a personal philosophy regarding serving -- should players be aggressive or not?

Serving Efficiency

This statistic determines the relative effectiveness of the serve based upon the opponent's pass. It is probably the single best indicator of an individual player's effectiveness. Serving efficiency is calculated according to the following point system:

• Four points for an ace serve;

• three points for a serve resulting in a pass that the setter cannot reach and another player sets;

• two points for a serve resulting in a pass that the setter sets, but not with the middle hitter option;

• one point for a serve resulting in a perfect pass, enabling the setter to run any offensive option; and

• zero points for a serving error (total points/number of serves = serving efficiency ratio).

Thus, if 24 serves earned 36 points, the service efficiency ratio would be 1.5 (36/24 = 1.5). Because passing is usually better at higher levels of play, the serving efficiency ratio typically is lower. For example, a normal ratio for the USA men's team is 1.5, while the ratio for collegiate women falls closer to 2.0.

> Serving Efficiency Ratio = (total points/number of serves)

Points Per Rotation

This statistic yields the average number of points scored during each rotation (term of service). Although the effectiveness of the individual's serve is of major importance, this statistic is also heavily influenced by the ability of the serving team to block, play defense and score points in transition.

Points per rotation is calculated from the official score sheet as follows:

• Count the total points scored by an individual or substitute and divide by the number of rotations (terms of service). (For example: ① ② ⓡ ⓡ ⑦ ⓡ ⓡ = three points scored in four rotations.)

•Individual formula: Three points scored/four rotations = .75 points/rotation.

•Team formula: Total points scored in game/total number of rotations = points per rotation. (For example: 15 points/25 rotations = .6 points/rotation).

The higher the level of play, the more rotations it takes to score points. The goal of the USA men's team is to win a game in 30 rotations or less and to score .5 points per rotation. The average for collegiate women's teams would be close to 25 rotations per game and .6 points per rotation. Again, remember that a low ratio may be attributed to more than just a weak server.

> Points Per Rotation = (total points scored in game/total number of rotations)

Ace to Error Ratio

This statistic compares aces to serving errors (total number of aces/

number of errors = ace-to-error ratio).

So, for example, if three aces are

Ace-to-Error Ratio = (total number of aces/number of errors)

served and errors are made, the formula calculates a .6 ace-to-error ratio. Generally, a team or individual wants more aces than errors. However, aggressive serving results in more errors, so a player who jump serves will commit significantly more errors. A ratio of 10 errors for every six aces, or a ratio of .6, would be considered very high for this skill. As another basis for comparison, the ace-to-error ratio should be about the same as the points-per-rotation ratio.

TEACHING THE JUMP SERVE

The sport of volleyball is unique because of the many acceptable methods of performing each technique (e.g. spiking approach, hand position for passing, setting style). This is certainly true for the jump serve. The material presented here represents one technique that has proven effective — others may be just as effective. It appears that the perfect candidate for learning the jump serve possesses these qualities:

The jump serve is not a skill that is quickly perfected. The coach and athlete must make a commitment of time and persistence -- consistency develops slowly.

- Good timing
- Controlled, efficient spiking approach
- Technically sound armswing
- Desire to learn the skill
- Ability to focus and concentrate.

The jump serve is not a skill that is quickly perfected. The coach and athlete must make a commitment of time and persistence—consistency develops slowly. The following descriptions illustrate the jump serve technique from start to finish.

STARTING POSITION (RIGHT-HANDED SERVER)

The server stands 10 to 15 feet back from the endline, squarely facing the net. Feet are in a front back stride position with the weight on the back (left) foot and the right foot slightly ahead. The ball is held at shoulder height, resting in the palm of the outstretched right hand. (We have found the one-handed toss to be more efficient and controlled.)

APPROACH AND TOSS

The approach is begun by simultaneously stepping forward (weight transfer) with the right foot and lowering the right arm in preparation for the toss. As the right arm moves upward to release the ball the left is moving forward for the second step of the approach. The ball is released with a slight flip of the wrist off the ends of the fingertips at head height, as the left foot comes through. By releasing the ball off the fingertips the server accomplishes two important actions. First, topspin (forward spin) is imparted to the toss, helping to keep the ball traveling in a consistent path; second, the ball will travel upward, as well as forward, over the end- line. It is important that the ball be tossed forward, in front of the server and in line with the hitting arm. The height of the toss varies with each individual — generally, it should be 10 to 15 feet.

TAKE-OFF AND JUMP
After the ball is released and while the last two steps of the approach are taken, the arms begin a downswing then backswing type motion similar to the spiking approach. Just as in a spike approach, the right foot plants and the left foot closes. Note that the feet should leave the floor slightly behind the end line. As the step-close steps are taken, the arms begin a forceful upswing. When the feet leave the floor the arms should already be up, with the left arm extended and pointing toward the ball and the right arm drawn back in a cocked position. The body is moving forward (over the end line) "chasing" the toss. The back is arched as the shoulders rotate and "open."

CONTACT
It is essential that the approach and jump put the body in a position under the descending ball. The armswing begins with the elbow high and leading the shoulder rotation back to a "closed" position. The armswing is made as the ball drops to a contact position slightly behind the hitting shoulder. The ball is contacted with an open hand. Initially, the heel of the hand contacts the ball slightly below the center point of the ball. Immediately after this, the whole hand makes contact with the ball by snapping the wrist and extending the arm over the ball. This type of contact results in a topspin serve — the ball travels in a relatively straight trajectory, then drops dramatically after it crosses the net. Increasing the speed of the armswing will increase the velocity of the ball. The body should be in the air, moving forward and well past the end line.

FOLLOW-THROUGH AND LANDING
After contact, the fully extended right arm continues through its full range of motion. The legs are pulled forward and prepare for landing. When the toes of both feet make contact with the floor, the knees bend to cushion the landing. A good jump server will land 4 to 6 feet into the court.

ADDITIONAL CONSIDERATIONS
Placement
As players gain consistency and become more proficient at the jump serve, they can work at serving to specific areas. Obviously, this technique is more difficult to control.

Fatigue
Assuming your athletes are well-conditioned, fatigue should not seriously limit their ability to use this serve throughout a long match. Many coaches overestimate the energy required to perform this skill and under-

"When analyzing how we teach a skill, it is probably best to look at what type of skill it is. Serving is really a single-action skill which should not be broken down and taught in pieces. Instead, repetitions of the whole skill should be done with the server focusing on one technical item of importance at a time. I call this single item focus training."

(John Dunning. Serve to win. *Coaching Volleyball*, March 1994.)

estimate the ability of their players. Players' ability to concentrate and focus on the jump serving technique is much more critical to success than their level of fatigue.

Coach Control

The coach should always remain in control of the team's service game. At a critical point in a game or match, the coach should make the decision about the type of serve to be used. The immediate past performance of the specific server and the coach's gut feeling will determine the final decision. Remember, it is important to show your players that you have confidence in their ability to serve aggressively in critical situations.

Psychological Factors

In addition to the statistical evaluations we discussed earlier, we believe that there are important psychological considerations in using the jump serve. Many times success with the jump serve early in a match can give the team a psychological edge that lasts throughout the match. The team becomes more aggressive and confident. That aggressive attitude is reflected in every phase of the game — digging, passing, blocking, hitting and serving. This type of behavior can be very intimidating to the opponents.

Stephanie Schleuder is the former head women's volleyball coach at the University of Minnesota in Minneapolis. Dorothy Franco-Reed is the head women's volleyball coach at the University of Alabama in Tuscaloosa, Ala. Both are USA Volleyball CAP certified coaches.

Serving and Scoring Efficiency

NICK CHERONIS

In volleyball, rotational statistics are a valuable source of information when determining whom to play and what rotation to use. In addition, serving holds a key to the potential efficiency of defense, and thus, scoring. Understanding the connection between serving, scoring and rotational analysis can make the difference in the success or failure of the team.

Photo: Long Beach State University

A coach needs to know several factors before settling on one serving strategy, from the opposition's reception patterns to who is blocking for your team.

BASIC STRATEGY

Calling "zones" is at the heart of serving strategy. This aspect of coaching has become very popular at all levels of play. Much like a catcher in baseball calling pitches for a pitcher, the coach can manipulate the opposition's serve receive pattern by serving to weaknesses in a pattern or weaknesses to particular passers.

There are several reasons why one would serve to a particular zone. The most obvious reason is to serve to a fundamentally weak passer. However, with volleyball becoming more specialized, weak passers are becoming a rare breed.

Coaches are using two-, three- and four player serve receive patterns in order to counter serving zone strategies. Thus, a coach needs to know several other factors before settling on one serving strategy:
- the opposition's reception patterns
- the opposition's offensive tendencies
- who is serving for your team
- who is blocking for your team
- what are your serving goals.

Reception patterns frequently leave unprotected areas of the court for which to serve, especially in the age of passing specialization. Many believe that two passers cannot effectively cover the entire court on serve receive, but even three or four passers will leave vulnerable areas in almost every pattern.

Offensive tendencies such as an "x" play, the slide attack or the "31" combination, can be vulnerable to particular serves. This is particularly true when a primary passer is involved in the tendency.

Servers will always have a "favorite" zone. Building serving flexibility or training players to serve effectively to all areas of the court is a key to long-term scoring success. However, players will always favor a particular area and generally that "favorite" zone is a very effective serve.

It is also important to know your team's blocking strengths and weaknesses. Many times serving down the line (zone 5) will yield a left side attack. Thus, it becomes imperative that your team hold a blocking advantage in that situation.

Lastly, it is important to establish serving goals. Players need feedback as to how these serving strategies work and if they are working. Conversely, coaches also need immediate feedback to determine if their serving strategies are proving to be effective. Most coaches and players understand these alternative strategies; however, it is usually guesswork as to its effectiveness. Typically, adjusting the strategies during a match is usually done without much statistical support.

"We in volleyball certainly need servers who can consistently throw strikes -- just in the court at some lower levels or to the specific zone called at higher levels. After all, we do not have the luxury of four balls before something bad happens. A screaming jump serve right into the arms of a passer will usually result in a good pass. Thus, we try to serve in seams between passers and usually never directly at a player, at the passer, at the point of the W serve receive or at a passer standing too shallow in the court. This is analogous to jamming a hitter crowding the plate with a high fastball."

(Shang Hsiung, Baseball and the volleyball serve," *Coaching Volleyball*, October/November 1990, 16.)

Establishing serving goals is the key to successful serving.

DEVELOPING A STATISTICAL SERVING SYSTEM

As you have read, it is imperative to develop a serving chart or a "road map" that immediately tells a coach where they have been and where they want to go. The serving chart illustrated in Table 1 is a chart that has been developed over several years. It gives information as to what zone has been called, how many setting options the second contact player had and the result of the play.

Depending upon the level of play, one may wish to track the accuracy of the serve. At our level (NCAA Division I), accuracy is not as significant a factor as effectiveness. Instead, we are more interested in how many options a particular serve yields and if that resulted in a point.

In Table 1, the numbers listed across the top are the number of times the opposition has gone through its rotation. Four complete rotations in one game is a fairly high number for our level. Higher levels of play, particularly the men's game, will frequently yield this many rotations because of the increased side-out ability.

The first number in the charting sequence for each player is the called zone. A capital "I" signifies that the player was given her "favorite" zone signal. It is important that a player focus on a zone rather than adjust getting the ball in. Concentration and staying focused are keys to consistent and effective serving.

The second number is the number of options the second contact player had after the initial pass. This is based on a potential of three total options, regardless if the setter is front or back row. Thus, the following system seems to work well:

- "1" signifies that only one option was available to set after the pass.
- "2" signifies two options were available.
- "3" signifies that three options were usable (including a dump attack if the setter is in the front row).
- "0" signifies that no setting options were available.

It should be noted that a "0" pass does not necessarily mean an ace serve; it simply means that no setting options were available. In Table 1, Laura (rotation 3) served a zero option pass that resulted in a free ball (FB). Bigs (rotation 2) served a zero option pass that resulted in an over-pass kill (OP) and Janene (rotation 4) served a free ball situation which we did not convert into a point. A certain amount of analysis on free ball transition and aggressiveness on overpasses can be derived from this information.

The final character in the sequence is the result of the play. Point (P), side out (S) and error (E) are used to determine scoring efficiency per rotation. All of this information can be used in aiding the decision making process in calling zones. For example, in Bigs' case, two short zones were called prior to the deep "6" zone, which resulted in the overpass for a point.

TABLE 1 - SERVING CHART

Name/Rotation	1	2	3	4	OP/SE	Att-Opt-Pt-E
1. Laura	1-2-S	I-3-S	(fb) 5-0-P 5-0-S	5-2-P 5-3-S	2.00/.333	6-12-2-0
2. Bigs	3-1-S	2-1-P (op) 6-0-P 3-1-S	2-2-S	5-3-S	1.33/.333	6-8-2-0
3. Janene	(ace) 5-0-P	Tina 5-3-S	Tina 5-2-P	(fb) 5-0-S	1.75/.500 Tina 2.33/.333	5-7-3-0 Tina 3-7-1-0
4. Karlin	1-3-P	I-3-P I-3-S	1-2-S 1-1-P I-2-S	I-1-P	2.14/.571	7-15-4-0
5. Amy	6-E	I-1-P	6-3-S I-3-S	NA	2.33/.333	3-7-1-1
6. Kim	I-3-P	5-3-S I-2-S	5-3-P 5-1-S	NA	2.40/.400	5-12-2-0

LEGEND:
OP   Opposition Passing
SE   Scoring Efficiency
Att   Attempts
Opt   Zero Option Passes
Pt   Points Scored
E   Service Errors

5 - 1 - S

1) Zone called by the coach   2) No. options available to setter   3) Result of the play

In Janene's case, a "5" zone resulted in an ace the first time around. This information was used for the fourth time around to gain a free ball opportunity toward the end of the game.

As far as making adjustments between games, two numbers are very important:

1. Opposition passing (options divided by total attempts) and
2. scoring efficiency (points scored divided by the total attempts plus errors).

In the first two rotations, the scoring efficiency is the same (.333). In other words, every three times we serve in those rotations, we score one point. However, the opposition is only passing 1.33 in the second rotation, compared to 2.00 in the first. Logic would suggest we should be scoring more efficiently in the second rotation than the first because of a more effective serve. Thus, changes in personnel or defensive strategies may be in order.

Also, our defensive specialist, Tina, is allowing 2.33 options, while her rotation is only scoring .333 efficiency. Janene, on the other hand, is holding the opposition to a 1.40 passing and is scoring at .600. This suggests leaving Janene in to serve and bringing Tina in for sideout situations.

Similar situations can be observed for individual players as well as varying strategies. Generally, a match needs to be played out a little further before sweeping generalizations can be made. However, these are indications of what is happening in the match with regards to scoring. Scoring efficiency and opposition passing for each rotation can be analyzed post-match to determine various blocking and defensive needs.

Generally, aces are not a primary goal in serving. Therefore, it is imperative for players to get positive recognition if their serve results in a free ball or an overpass.

In Table 2, serving statistics can be used to set individual and team goals. Generally, aces are not a primary goal in serving. Therefore, it is imperative for players to get positive recognition if their serve results in a free ball or an overpass.

The categories in Table 2 stand for serving attempts, not including errors (SA); number of options passed (OPT); the opposition's passing average (OPT/A); the number of points scored on that player's serve (Pt Scd); the number of times the serve resulted in no options (0's); the number of times the serve resulted in three options (3's) and the number of errors (E). Errors need to be in a separate category because we are calculating the opposition's passing average; consequently, the number of errors needs to be included when figuring error ratio, also known as serving percentage (E/ATT+E) and scoring efficiency (PTS/ATT+E). The goals listed will change over the course of a season depending upon the team's

TABLE 2 - SERVING STATISTICS

Name	SA	Opt	Opt/A	PrScd	O's	3's	E
Kris	30	44	1.47	15	7	5	1
Bigs	564	883	1.57	317	99	134	31
Steph	153	244	1.59	79	35	44	23
Graham	288	461	1.60	149	48	65	21
Janene	143	242	1.69	79	26	48	20
Jackie	207	359	1.73	105	27	59	22
Kim	164	285	1.74	74	22	48	27
Karlin	255	462	1.81	132	28	79	11
Tina	291	535	1.84	156	40	101	27
Red	115	216	1.88	55	11	44	19
Amy	385	740	1.92	191	41	134	30
Heidi	15	36	2.40	7	0	9	2
Totals	2610	4507	1.73	1359	384	770	234

Category	Figures	Goals	Your %
Pts/Att+E	0.478	0.50	_____
Err/Att+E	0.083	0.07	_____
Opt Pass	1.730	1.60	_____
O's/Att	0.147	0.18	_____
3's/Att	0.295	0.30	_____

Data complied from 1990 Southwest Missouri State women's volleyball team.

Mary Frances Heishman (1989) believes that "with help, any player can improve performance with a preservice routine. The routine should be planned by the player with guidance from the coach, who can provide an outline and possible techniques to be used in the routine. The coach should remind the player to use the routine at practice and in matches. No single routine is good for every player; each routine should be matched to the individual. Athletes should feel comfortable with their routines.

Most routines should include the following elements:

•Relaxation procedures to lower and control anxiety.

•Mental strategies to achieve an optimal level of readiness.

•A combination of mental and physical strategies to manage stress.

•A consistent physical starting point.

A sample routine is as follows:

1. Prior to ball possession: step away from service area; relax, take three deep breaths; shrug and relax shoulders; concentrate on a weak receiver.

2. As the ball is rolled to you and you are waiting for the official's signal, bounce the ball two times; concentrate on the ball level; keep your thoughts directed toward the center of gravity; say "I am in control."

3. After the official whistles for service, bounce the ball once; take a deep breath; visualize the ball going to the target; use positive self-talk "I am a great server."

4. At the actual service, lift the ball and punch center back.

(Mary Frances Heishman. Improve consistency with preservice routines. *Coaching Volleyball*, December/ January) 1989, 18-19.)

serving ability.

Provided to the right of the team goals is a place for each player to figure her respective percentage. It is meaningful to emphasize that the player does not have complete control over some of the outcomes. For example, scoring points is a function of the defense and its ability to transition from defense to offense. By holding the opposition's passing average down and keeping the error ratio low, the ability to score points will eventually follow.

You may want to calculate the scoring efficiency and the error ratio for each player (the first and second percentages). It is no coincidence that four of the top five opposition passing leaders are also scoring efficiency leaders on the team.

As coaches, we are constantly telling our players to serve aggressively and to serve in the court. This article illustrates how statistics show your players the importance of effective serving. It also shows which rotations are doing the best job of scoring points.

Obviously, serving to zones holds tremendous advantages in changing the momentum of matches and in scoring points. Most serving statistics focus on accuracy, which can be helpful; however, it is scoring points efficiently that ultimately wins matches.

Nick Cheronis is the assistant women's volleyball coach at the University of Florida and was a USA Youth national team coach in 1994.

The topspin serve and the jump serve can be used as two very effective offensive weapons given the server has mastered the techniques involved in the serves. Since both serves have numerous techniques inherent within, we must first address the techniques of the topspin serve.

The topspin serve is a great serve to use as a changeup and to catch the opponent off guard. It is a serve that is hit with a great deal of speed, force and spin, causing it to move very quickly over the net and drop rapidly to the floor on the opponent's side. One drawback that the topspin serve has is that its trajectory from the server is very easily determined. However, its speed, spin and sudden dropping action give your opponent little time to react to it, especially when used interspersed with other servers.

The topspin serve, according to Collins, is great serve to use as a changeup and to catch the opponent off guard.

TEACHING CUES FOR THE TOPSPIN SERVE

1. Service stance for the topspin serve is basically the same as for the overhead floater serve. The force that creates the topspin is the position of the hand at contact and the subsequent follow through.

2. The topspin server must bend backward prior to contact. In order for this to happen successfully, the toss must be higher than for a floater. The toss must also be slightly closer to the server and in a direct line with the hitting arm. **Cue: "high toss."**

3. Contact of the ball is made on the lower section of the ball with the heel of the open hand. **Cue: "Hit the bottom 1/4 of the ball."**

4. The ball is hit forcefully upward and forward with a strong, quick snap of the wrist, bringing the fingers up the back and over the top of the ball. This action generates the topspin. **Cue: "Snap the wrist."**

5. Weight transfer from the back foot to the front foot occurs at contact.

6. Follow through is the same as for a down-the-line spike with full range of motion throughout the serve. **Cue: "Follow through."**

The jump serve has many variables involved in the correct execution, thereby making it a rather difficult serve to master. However, once mastered, a jump serve is a superb accessory to have in one's repertoire because it allows the jump server to contact the ball higher, generating a lower trajectory. This lower trajectory from the server makes it more difficult for the opponent to pass this serve effectively.

Once mastered, a jump serve is a superb accessory to have in one's repertoire because it allows the jump server to contact the ball higher, generating a lower trajectory. This lower trajectory from the server makes it more difficult for the opponent to pass this serve effectively.

The jump serve requires a higher toss and a lateral jump in the air. Contact with the ball is the same as with the topspin serve. The jump-served ball must have a sufficient amount of topspin or the ball may end up out-of-bounds. The biggest problem with the jump serve is the height of the toss, which can only be mastered with repeated practice.

According to Collins, the cues outlined here will help any player master the topspin and jump serves.

TEACHING KEYS FOR THE JUMP SERVE

1. The start position must be determined by first making the approach, without a ball (in an effort to gauge the preferred distance behind the service line to execute the serve without foot faulting.)

2. After the start position has been determined, the toss must be mastered. The toss is initiated with two hands.

3. The ball is tossed well into the air and toward the endline on the second step of the approach. **Cue: "Very high toss in front of you."**

4. The serving motion is the same as the four-step spike approach which ends with a powerful vertical jump. **Cue: "Spike approach."**

5. The hand contact with the ball should be the heel-snap contact below the midpoint of the ball, just as in the topspin. **Cue: "Hit the bottom 1/4 of the ball" and "snap the wrist."**

6. Follow through includes a full range of motion of the serving arm and landing well inside the service line. **Cue: "Follow through."**

Both the topspin serve and the jump serve are tough to master in terms of efficiency. However, once mastered, both are highly effective.

Sandra D. Collins is the head girls' varsity volleyball coach at Bethlehem Central High School in Delmar, N.Y., and is a USA Volleyball CAP certified coach.

Section III: The Set

Volleyball is among the purest of all team sports. It is virtually impossible for one player to dominate the game as a great running back in football or a tremendous shooter in basketball. Yet, because of the nature of these sports and the number of contacts afforded the setter, that person carries a dramatically over-weighted value. Few teams in football reach their potential or any measure of success without a great quarterback and, likewise, few volleyball teams can perform to their abilities without the great setter or setters.

These players come close to making one-third of all ball contacts by a team. But more important is that they usually direct the middle contact of the normal sequence in volleyball events. Between the pass and the attack, the setter is in control. The setter makes or breaks the hitters, builds or destroys confidence in the passers, establishes tempo for a team's play, develops rhythm for the offense and generally runs the show. Indeed, the setter is the most critical person on the team. A coach must put more thought into selection of setters and more time into their training than any other function.

According to Beal, the setter must exhibit unequaled self-confidence and must believe he or she can deliver the required set every time.

SETTER SELECTION

Primarily, a team will take on the personality of the coach. It will normally reflect the coach's emotional highs, lows and evenness in temperament. However, the next in line to influence the emotional and psychological characteristics of a team is the setter. Careful thought must be given to non-physical traits in selecting the setter. Briefly, look for:

The setter is the most critical person on the team. A coach must put more thought into selection of setters and more time into their training than any other function.

1. Intelligence—the ability to assimilate information from the sidelines and translate it to effective action and the ability to perceive the game in total.

2. Self-confidence—total belief that you have the best "hands" in the business and simply cannot make a ball-handling error. The setter must know that he/she can deliver the required set, can get to every ball and can lead the team to victory.

3. The "sponge" characteristic—the setter accepts responsibility for all hitting mistakes. He/she will constantly seek feedback from hitters, trying to give them exactly what they want. Setters must never get into confrontations with hitters. Remember, all sets the hitter successfully kills are "great sets" and all hitting errors and stuff blocks are results of poor sets.

4. Emotional stability—this is always within the framework of the coach. But basically, the setter must be very stable and not exhibit dramatic highs and lows, which could easily affect the team. The setter must be a cheerleader when things are good and avoid depression when things are bad.

Certainly, there are many other abilities and characteristics important to setters, but overall strong leadership in a player who understands the game and executes the coach's wishes is of top priority.

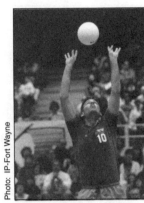

A great pair of hands on a tall player makes for a very good setter.

With regard to physical traits in a setter, look for the following:
1. Outstanding general athletic ability—the ability to win, plus quickness, power, size and perception.
2. A great pair of hands—a great touch on the ball and a very quick release of the ball; total control of the delivery of every set.
3. Good size—do not necessarily make your small players setters.
4. Good agility and body awareness.
5. Good spatial orientation.

THE OVERALL SETTER

Now, the trick is to meld the two sets of traits (physical and psychological) to select the best overall profile for setters.

The best setters clearly understand their role on the team and how best to function on the floor. The coach must constantly verbalize and train the setter to make the appropriate choices and selections.

The setter's primary role is to always deliver a "good" set. The good set implies several qualities. This is a truly hittable set for each attacker (i.e., what hitters think they can handle in any situation). The good set will give the attacker optimum possibilities to succeed on his or her own skills. The good set is truly "hittable," based on location.

If the setter can always accomplish the "good' set, then the role expands to become a "smart" setter. The smart set will match your strengths to opponent weaknesses; will feed the "hot" attacker; will take advantage of what your offense does best; and will effectively carry out the thoughts and plans of the coach. The smart setter is the second progression once your player(s) have mastered the technical side of delivering the ball accurately and effectively. If you have a player who has achieved the first two roles of a setter, you are a great coach. Your setter is probably not directly winning for your team, but he or she is never losing for your team.

The final stage in the development of setters and their priority hierarchy in delivering the ball is for the setter to assume the burden for defeating the block. This is done by "tricky" or "cute" setting. The setter's objectives can now include deception in an effort to allow hitters to be working against less than the well-formed two- or three-player block.

I want to emphasize that this is far and away the lowest and last priority for the setter. A tricky set which fools the block but is not hittable is worthless. Generally, this role is beyond the skills of most setters and will only lead to unnecessary errors. Your offense must always live within the skills and abilities of your players – – and especially your setters. One of the cardinal principals of coaching is never to ask your players to perform skills or tactics beyond their abilities. You must use their existing skills and build upon them and add new ones.

Setting is very much a percentage skill that will hopefully lead to a minimum of errors in your offense. Therefore, remember to be technically perfect first, smart second, and then, maybe occasionally tricky.

This is the most specialized training that occurs on your team. You must place your setter(s) in more situations and acquaint them with more potential situations than everyone else. As stated earlier, they control more of the game than anyone else, so they should receive more attention. The following concepts should be kept in mind in developing and honing a setter.

REPETITION

There is no key to success like repetition. The setter must touch as many balls per practice as possible. If you have all players on your team performing all skills equally, you are not effectively training your players. The setter must set more than anything else. The center blockers must spend more time blocking, the big hitters need practice there, etc.

POSITIONAL VARIETY

The setters must learn to set from all body positions. This means jump setting, running forward, running backward, rolling on the floor, underhand setting, setting balls coming out of the net, one-hand setting, backcourt setting, setting balls with lots of spin, setting balls moving very fast at them and setting balls coming from very high. The possibilities are almost limitless. This is crucial so the setters will react instinctively to any situation during the game. You cannot train your setters by merely having them set from a stationary situation.

There is a secondary effect of having the setter trained to emergency setting tactics and that is that the hitters become familiar with attacking these sets and they learn the setter's capabilities. It is certainly best to simulate game situations with all drills and this implies the setter setting to hitters.

SETTING TACTICS

You must train the setter according to game situations. This means that you construct a situation and let the setter react. For example, it is very good to set left when the setter must move to the right and vice versa. The middle blockers usually will anticipate a set in the direction the setter is moving and it is a good tactic to make the blockers move a long way. This must be trained in drill situations. You would like to train the setters to be able to see the center blocker. Therefore, you must drill them with the center blockers making designed moves. If the setter is forced to jump set, you should train him/her to set anyplace but the middle, etc. These tactical considerations must be trained.

SPATIAL ORIENTATION

The setter must know where he/she is at all times. You have several points to consider in this training. First, we must train the setter to see the ball, lose sight of it, find it again and then set. These drills involve the setter seeing the ball, then executing some skill (dive, roll, jump, spin, etc.), find the ball and set. Second, the setter must learn to start without seeing the ball, then find it and set. This involves the setter starting blind,

According to Brassey-Iversen (1995), the setter has to have the highest stamina of any player on the team.

"When I think about the patterns that a setter runs in a game -- penetrating from serve receive, going to cover, going back to defense, coming back in to set -- she is running all over the court. In the course of a five-game match, you have probably run a couple of miles. You have to be quick and accurate the whole time."

(Brassey-Iversen, Laurel and Dan McDonough. Demands of the setting position. *Critical Thinking on Setter Development*, 1995, 50.)

58

finding the ball after it is in play and setting. Another type of spatial orientation concerns the setter's ability to know the dimensions of the court, especially from the perimeters and beyond. Essentially, we are talking about setting long distances after moving great distances and accurately setting to the correct spot on the court.

> If the ball is consistently off in one direction, you should check your setter's alignment. Good direction starts with the feet, but the shoulders are more critical. The feet dictate motion, while the shoulders dictate direction.

To complete the training of the setter, you must give him/her the proper authority and control. Setters must have the freedom to call the plays and run the offense, or at least make appropriate changes even if the hitters call your plays. The setter must establish an effective range so the hitters know which balls the setter will set and which set they must help with. The setter must quarterback the team and that is a joint project of the personalities of the setter and the coach.

According to Beal, it is critical that setters take the ball from a consistently high position to allow hitters to judge the speed of the release.

TECHNICAL ASPECTS

I will briefly describe some of the basic flaws common to setting, what to look for and how to correct them. Setting is a very complex motor skill that the slightest miscalculation can destroy. It will be impossible to go over all aspects, but here are several crucial elements.

1. The setter should be stopped when he/she contacts the ball. If the ball is never going where the setter wants it to (it always drifts or comes up short) it is likely the setter is moving through the set. Certainly, it is unavoidable at times, but usually it is not. By all means, the setter must be stopped at the moment of contact.

2. The setter must face the target; this means with the upper body (especially the shoulders). If the ball is consistently off in one direction, you should check your setter's alignment. Good direction starts with the feet, but the shoulders are more critical. The feet dictate motion, while the shoulders dictate direction.

3. The ball must be contacted at a high point. This is critical for a consistent release and the ability to go in every possible direction with the ball. A high point means in front of the face above the eyebrows. It is very critical that the setters take the ball from a consistently high position to allow the hitters to judge accurately the speed of release for good timing. An inconsistent contact point means different trajectories to the same sets and poor timing for the hitters.

4. The ball must be released from the setter's midline. This is of concern, especially when the ball is passed to the setter close to the net. It is common to reach out to set the ball and contact it before it arrives at the midline of the setter. This causes the jerking of the ball across the body and a set that will be too "tight" or cross the net. A setter with good hand absorption will rarely have this problem.

5. The set should be made off the back foot, actually pushing through the ball to maintain an effective line of force from the floor, through the total body, to the point of ball release. The outside foot (fur-

thest from the net) is normally the back foot. Using the foot furthest from the net causes a slight drift toward the net and this type of ball is much easier to hit for the spiker. The setter must become comfortable with this foot position so he/she winds up stopping their feet planted correctly every time.

6. The setter should extend the arms completely on virtually every set. If the ball is released with the arms still bent, you have partially "jabbed" at the ball and not effectively followed through. A full follow-through will greatly increase accuracy.

I hope this discussion of setting has allowed you to see the complexity of the skill without inundating you with meaningless technicality. Remember, a team will rarely exceed the abilities of its setter(s); they are your most crucial players. Also, remember that there are no absolute rights and wrongs, only efficiencies and any individual's ability to perform successfully. Your guideline should always be performance and maximizing it for each individual on your team.

Doug Beal is the special assistant to the executive director/CEO for USA Volleyball and the 1984 Olympic Men's Volleyball Team head coach. That team earned a gold medal at the 1984 Olympic Games in Los Angeles, Calif. Beal is a USA Volleyball CAP certified coach.

Developing a
Setter-Centered Team

Developing a Setter-Centered Team Mary Ann Sprague

The setter's role on a volleyball team is constantly a topic of conversation, especially in terms of laying the foundation for a successful high school program. This is especially true when developing the young setter whom you have targeted to build your team around. How do you as a coach begin to train these athletes into true setters, the quarterback of the team?

This article addresses this issue, identifying four imperative steps a coach must employ in order to establish a setter-centered team. These steps include:

- honest communication
- education
- commitment to a program
- reaffirmation/praise.

Sprague believes a setter, especially at the younger levels, should not be reprimanded as often for mistakes because of the sheer number of ball contacts.

HONEST COMMUNICATION

There is little truth in a coach telling a team that all players will be treated the same. Accordingly, players must understand their roles, which need to be directed, redirected and communicated by the coaching staff. This is especially true in a setter-centered framework where this player will likely receive the most attention from the coaching staff. The all-important role of the setter need not be hidden from the rest of the team. In fact, it should be made clear from the very first practice or team meeting.

After making the decision to develop a setter-centered team, a coach should sit down with the setter(s) and clearly define what expectations you have of them. Be sure they understand their role:

- Take pressure off the rest of the team during practice and competition situations;
- increased time demands; and
- high levels of leadership and competitive behavior.

Conversely, tell the rest of the team that a large share of the practice time will be devoted to the setter position. Of course, emphasize that such attention will result in better sets for the hitters, a smoother transition game and a solid, confident offense.

It should also be made clear that the setter may not be reprimanded as often for making mistakes (at least not during team time). This is because the setter touches the ball much more often when compared to the rest of the team. Thus, the number of mistakes a setter makes will most likely be higher per game, but not necessarily proportional, to players in other positions.

These are examples of up-front, honest communication which need to be voiced at the start of a season. If the players understand the communication process during practice before they ever walk into the gymnasium, more time and energy can be spent on learning volleyball.

EDUCATION

Since the setter is deeply involved with all aspects of the game, he/she

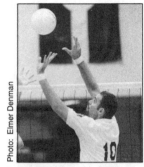

Photo: Elmer Denman

Educating the setter on position responsibilities is complicated, but crucial for a setter-centered team.

"The setter is the most important player within the team structure. The setter has to be the most consistent player on the court, day in and day out. The setter touches the ball once each time the ball is on their side. Therefore, he/she will have more contacts in initiating the attack per set than any other player on the team. This, when done at a satisfactory and consistent level, will give the team the stability that it needs to have potential for performance. Winning and losing can have direct relationships to the abilities of the player chosen for this position. The importance of the "play maker" can readily be seen in the situations where a good setter has made a good attack occur when the pass was not optimum."

(Lorne Sawula, Ph.D. (1995). Basic technique training. *Critical Thinking on Setter Development*.)

has to be well-educated in two major areas—"our" side of the net and "their" side of the net.

Educating your setter on the position responsibilities is complicated. The setter needs to know the hitters well. Are they left- or right-handed? Can they use blockers or do they need open court to hit well? Tight to the net or off? Pushed out or inside?

The back row also has to be understood by the setter, especially in a 6-2 offense or the back end of a 5-1. The defensive or free ball transition for the setter to the net is anything but simple. If the setter is involved in the first defensive contact (or free ball), he/she must know where to play the ball and how to support the play from that moment on. Whereas everyone else knows where to pass the ball because the target never changes, the setter has to know where the primary backup setter is and then assist accordingly.

One way of communicating second ball responsibilities which has proven effective at the high school level is for the setter to yell the name of the player who should take the second ball (e.g., "Jan, set"). Depending on the skill level of the player, a command indicating the type of set can be voiced (e.g., "Bob, set 5"). With these commands, the backup setter does not have to determine where the hitters are on the court. Instead, a high percentage set can be executed with confidence. Since the setter receives every kind of pass imaginable, they must learn how to play high percentage volleyball by making the "right" mistake versus the "wrong" mistake in a sticky situation.

Let us illustrate a possible scenario. Your right side hitter is left-handed, the outside hitter is drawn out of the play and the setter is in the middle hitter position. The setter is pulled to the middle of the court 15 feet off of the net by a bad pass. What to do?

In this particular case, the setter needs to know that a bump set back over the head is not a high percentage set, but may be the only option.

The "wrong" mistake is setting too far outside the court, especially with a left-handed attacker. The "right" mistake is setting the ball between the middle and right-side positions. Why? The right-side hitter can more easily attack this set instead of chasing a bad set with the wrong hand. If this attack option fails, this ball can easily be bumped over by another teammate if necessary.

A setter also needs to understand the decision-making process of playing high percentage volleyball versus running the team offense. If a setter is called for a double hit 50% of the time a dump is attempted, this attack should not be used for a sideout situation at a critical time in the match. A setter should stick to calling or making high percentage plays when confronted with the need of a sideout in a game-threatening situation.

The opponent's side of the net is probably the most difficult part of a setter's education. But there are several cardinal rules to increase this learning curve.

First, know your opponent's blockers, who they are in each rotation, and their blocking effectiveness. Second, look for ways to exploit the block by choosing the appropriate set. If you notice the middle blocker cheating toward the strong-side hitter, the time is right for a back set. Third, communicate to your hitters what kind of block they are up against (e.g., one-on-one, double, triple) and in response, adjust the set accordingly. For example, if the opponent sets a tough two-person block, the setter must take control by setting the ball slightly off the net to allow the hitter more working room around the block. If the opponent's block is late in closing, let the hitter know that attacking cross-court is a good option.

Applying this same procedure when analyzing the opponent's back-row defense, a setter must notice if anyone is defending against the tip or if there is a hole in their floor coverage. The coach should help identify these options, but the setter has the responsibility of taking advantage of these situations.

These aforementioned concepts, as logical as they might seem to coaches, are part of the setter's total educational process. Drills must be game-like in order for these situations to arise during practice. Coaches need to teach their setters to identify, evaluate and react to any situation in the best interest of the team.

COMMITMENT TO A STANDARD

Many times, coaches start the preseason with setter development high on the priority list, only to end the season never really accomplishing this objective. Coaches and players must stay on task. The top priority in your program has to be verified by what your team does every day in practice. Coaches need to realize that mistakes are bound to happen with a setter-centered team. Do not let this early season struggle influence your commitment. In time, it will get easier and the program will begin reaping the benefits.

REAFFIRMATION

The final step is reaffirmation. Three weeks into the season you will be attempting to convince yourself that building a setter-centered program was the right decision. Be prepared to convince your team at the same time. Reaffirm your decision by reacting consistently to the team gameplan. Basically, this means a great deal of patience. A coach cannot yell or scream when a "wrong" set is made. Education has to evolve. If the team goal during a match is to implement some higher-skilled offensive scheme, the setter should not be punished for mistakes made while attempting to run the offense. Instead, the feedback the setter needs is that of respect from the players and commitment from the coaching staff.

Learning will happen during practice and the coach's responsibility is to make sure this process happens. At game time, the coach can now switch from teacher to coach, watching the flow of the team and determining how much their setter has learned in practice. This evaluation

"The setter, the coach and the attacker can make or design the attacks. Teams use one or some combination of the above to run their offense. It is important for the coach to be in touch with the setter when on the court. Now that coaches can legally talk with the players on the court there will be more assistance given to the setter by the bench through verbal or hand signal forms. Yet, the coaches of the best teams do not call out every play during the match because the setter has to be able to have a feel for the game. Occasionally, the coach may want to remind the setter about some tactic. Watch that the setter does not always wait for you to say something. At a critical time the setter may be waiting for you or thinking about what you said and not feeling what should be set."

(Lorne Sawula, Ph.D. (1995). Communication for setters. *Critical Thinking on Setter Development*.)

Coaches need to teach their setters to identify, evaluate and react to any situation in the best interest of the team.

should help coaches plan future practices accordingly. Add a light heart and lots of laughs and you have developed a solid setter-centered team.

Mary Ann Sprague is the girls' volleyball coach with the Jacksonville Juniors Volleyball Association in Jacksonville, Fla., and is a USA Volleyball CAP certified coach.

Section IV: The Attack

Introductory Spiking Instruction: Make it Time-Efficient and Game-Related

Introductory Spiking Instruction: Make it Time-Efficient and Game-Related

DON SHONDELL

One of a coach's goals in creating drills is to be time efficient in construction and implementation. A continuous evaluation of the process is essential to determine how efficiently a particular drill, or drill progression, is in contributing to the mastery of the skill as measured by its efficient use in game situations.

Often, a coach constructs drills which are not game-like and result in the development of negative habits that must be broken before the skill can be efficiently used in competition. Examples of drills that might be counter productive are (1) standing at the wall, spiking down to the floor and having the ball rebound off the wall; (2) spiking a stationary ball; (3) hitting over a lowered net; (4) spiking into a net; and (5) spiking balls tossed almost on top of the net.

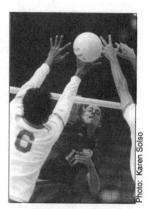

Developing consistency in spiking is crucial at any level.

The sequence for beginners should be game-related! The ball should be moving when hit, the net should be at regulation height and the execution of each drill should be done in a modified but game-like manner. The establishing of achievable goals is also critical to the enjoyment of the participants.

In teaching a fairly complex skill like spiking, however, I have found it beneficial to break down the skill into phases and take the entire group through specific elements using verbal commands and slow motion walk-throughs, without the use of a ball.

Examples would be the synchronization of the arm swing with the jump and the footwork used in the two-step (three-contact) approach. *In a left, right/left plant, the right-handed spiker starts with the weight on the right foot, steps with the left, hops off the left, turns 45° to the right and plants the feet well in front of the body with the right foot contacting the floor just prior to the contact of the left foot. This is called the two-step three-contact approach.

The sequence of drills I have found to be most effective in working with beginners of all ages is outlined below and will be explained later in detailed form.

SPIKING SEQUENCE FOR BEGINNERS

1. Purpose of the spike.
2. Arm swing (without ball).
3. Ball relationship synchronization of the arm swing and timing of jump (with ball using 4-foot toss).
4. Hitting a two ball* from 4 feet off the net with no approach, stressing the importance of high elbow and wrist snap (4-foot toss).
5. Two-step footwork (without ball).
6. Two-step footwork, pause and hitting a two ball (4-foot toss).
7. Two-step footwork and hitting a two ball (6-foot toss).
(*Two ball - a ball tossed four feet higher than the spiker's height in drills 3, 4 and 6, but 6 feet higher in drill 7).

According to Shondell, a beginning spiker's goal is to attack the ball across the net consistently and into the back third of the court.

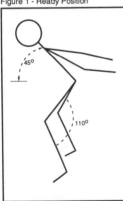

Figure 1 - Ready Position

PURPOSE OF THE SPIKE

A beginning spiker's goal is to attack the ball consistently across the net and into the back third of the court. Velocity is not important at the beginning level. Re-emphasize that success of each spike will be dependent on whether or not the ball passes over the net and lands in the back third of the court. The acceptance of this simple concept by each player is a critical first step in developing consistency in spiking.

THE ARM SWING (WITHOUT BALL)

The second concept involves utilization of an aggressive armswing when preparing to jump and spike. Beginners frequently are not aware that the armswing can assist the jumper in adding additional height to the jump if both arms have been aggressively swung forward and upward prior to the spiker leaving the floor. Conversely, if the arms are swung late or not swung at all, they become a dead counterweight that will be added to the body weight as the jumping muscles prepare to propel the body into the air.

This arm action should be practiced with the entire group of learners assuming a ready-to-jump position. In this position, the following factors should be stressed:

1. Feet are spread to shoulder width. Weight is on inside of feet.
2. Hips and legs are flexed approximately 110°.
3. Body bends forward at the waist to form a 45° angle with the floor
4. Arms are simultaneously extended and rotated backward (see Figure 1).

READY POSITION

After visually checking the "ready" position of all of the subjects, remind them to concentrate on an aggressive arm swing. Repeat this several times using the following verbal cues: (1) feet spread shoulder width, legs bent, weight on inside of feet; (2) arms back; (3) trunk forward 45°, "ready"; (4) fast armswing; (5) jump; and (6) prior to landing, wide base and cushion. Stress that cushioning reduces landing impact on the knees and back, while a wide base will assist in maintaining equilibrium and minimizing net and center-line violations.

BALL RELATIONSHIP AND TIMING OF JUMP

Another major concept of spiking, which often results in frustration to the coach and learner, is developing a proper relationship to the ball and timing. The two are covered simultaneously because both are directly related to spiking the ball consistently with control across the net into the back third of the court.

In my early training, Jim Coleman, current director of the USA Volleyball National Teams Training Center, had a theory on teaching the spike that I could not then accept. Coleman's theory was to teach the beginner to spike away from the net. Like so many young coaches, I felt this made the process more difficult and, in terms of logic, it made more sense to move the beginner closer to the net and perhaps to help him/her get it over, even lowering the net. I found, eventually, that my method did work in a drill, but it did not transfer to success in game situations. First, in a game, no one was allowed to pull the net down for the hitter, and secondly, the beginning setter had little margin of error in setting. Consequently, many of the balls were set on, or even over, the net, resulting in a net error by the attacker or a free ball for the opponent on an overset. A third problem was no one knew how to attack balls set away from the net; thus, the hitter would either hit the deep set into the net or out of bounds or free-ball pass the ball to the opponent. I soon found the "set on the net" technique was not the best method and, coupled with the now-popular tactic of attacking from the back row, the deep set theory of Coleman's began to make more sense.

I am recommending that you teach beginners to spike a ball tossed a minimum of 4 feet away from the net. To add to initial success, I also recommend "no approach spiking," and attacking a ball tossed straight up in front of the spiker to a height 4 feet higher than the spiker's standing height. The shortest player, contacting a ball 4 feet from the net can easily, by keeping the elbow high, angle the ball over the net into the opponent's court with the net at regulation height.

The straight-up toss allows the players to toss for one another because it is an easily controlled toss requiring no footwork by the attacker. I have also found that many beginners do not know when to jump. By tossing 4 feet higher than the top of the spiker's head and telling him/her to jump as soon as the rising ball begins to drop, it provides a specific timing cue.

As for ball/spiker relationship, the tosser is to stand 4 feet from the net, facing the left sideline. The spiker is to stand 5 feet from the net, so as to contact the ball 1 foot in front of the spiking shoulder (see Figure 2).

This deep-hit, low-toss drill will allow three lines at the net. The coach gives verbal commands so he/she can visually check to be certain the drill is being done properly.

Command cues are (1) legs bent 110°; (2) feet spread shoulder width; (3) arms back (and on toss); (4) swing arms; (5) jump, reach and catch; (6) wide base; and (7) cushion.

> I am recommending that you teach beginners to spike a ball tossed a minimum of 4 feet away from the net.

Figure 2 - Toss and Spike Without Approach Drill (top view)

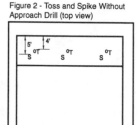

S - Subject
°T - Tosser With Ball

JUMPING AND CATCHING A TOSSED BALL

The coach must demonstrate to the tossers how to hold and toss the ball. The tosser will stand 4 feet from the net, facing the sideline with the arms extended in front of the body. The ball rests in the open hands. The tossing process is actually a lifting process, similar to the toss in tennis, but done with both hands. The coach should demonstrate where to stand and how to toss the ball in front of one of the subjects. Remind the group of the height of the toss - 4 feet higher than the subject's head - and if the ball were allowed to drop to the floor, it should land 1 foot in front of the spiker's hitting shoulder.

Have tossers practice the toss several times (the first person in line is the tosser and he/she will toss for everyone in the line). When each player

Photo: Laura Vaughn

Shondell believes spiking is not a difficult skill to learn if you simplify the process.

in line has taken a turn, the person at the head of the line becomes the next tosser and the previous tosser goes to the end of the line.

The coach's command will be "tosser ready." On this command, the tosser, facing the sideline, reaches out with both arms and holds the ball at chest height in front of the spiker. At this point, the coach talks the spiker into the correct "spiker-ready" position (legs bent 110°, feet spread shoulder width and arms back).

The tosser tosses the ball straight up to a height 4 feet higher than the spiker's height and 1 foot in front of the spiker's shoulder. As the ball begins to drop, the spiker swings both arms rapidly forward and upward and then jumps, catching the ball at the highest point possible with the arms extended overhead. Reaching upward for the ball with extended arms is important!

Repeat with the same person a second time. The attacker catches the ball and rotates to the end of line. The next person in line moves to the proper spot near the tosser and assumes the spiker-ready position.

The most common errors are:

1. Toss - too low, or too high, or not straight up and down;

2. attacker - not assuming leg flex position. Arms not back when waiting for toss or not swinging arms properly (straight back and straight up);

3. spikers not jumping straight up from where they stand. Instead, they are taking a little jump or step forward and coming down directly under the ball instead of 1 foot behind it; and

4. incorrect landing.

A visual demonstration is necessary before putting the subjects through any of the drills. Point out the cue words to be used during the demonstration.

TOSS AND HIT WITH NO APPROACH

The next phase is begun as soon as the players have had success with "toss and catch." Pick a demonstrator. I suggest using a small, average athlete because the subject will have immediate success and this will encourage those without great height or physical ability to have confidence that they can do it. Explain that it usually takes three trials for the average beginner to get the ball over the net and deep on the court. Explain that instead of jumping and catching the low-tossed ball, the spiker will now swing both arms up, and as he/she leaves the floor, flex the hitting arm; using the palm of the open hand, hit the ball upward and over the net. Keep the non-hitting arm in the air on this drill.

The secret is an aggressive armswing, high elbow on the striking arm and an open hand with fingers spread and aggressive wrist snap.

Give the subject a good toss and a lot of encouragement and the attacker will hit it over on one of the three trials. If the ball goes into net, restress the high-elbow concept.

In this drill, the player will chase the ball after it clears the net. The second person in line should have a ball ready to hand to the tosser. The drill should move rapidly. The toss in this drill is the same as it was in the toss and catch drill. As the entire line hits, the person at the front of the line becomes the new tosser, with the previous tosser moving to the end of the line. If the drill is not going well, re-demonstrate, emphasizing the cue words. Use a different demonstrator.

THE 45° ANGLE PRELIMINARY POSITION - JUMP, TURN AND SWING

After success has been attained in the toss and catch drill, demonstrate a 45° degree angle to the net plant position. Explain that the rotation of the body when hitting gives the attacker more power in contacting the ball (as in throwing a softball for distance). The non-hitting arm is swung up and along with the hitting arm, but is dropped and pulled back during the spiking action.

Have the group spread out and practice the "jump and turn" to the instructor's command:

1. Body at 45° angle to the net;
2. ready position - arms back; and
3. swing arms, jump and turn. The subject will be facing the net when landing after contact (your only concern about the non-hitting arm is to be certain it is swung up and pointing at the ball prior to contact; then allow it to descend naturally during the hitting action).

THE TWO-STEP APPROACH (WITHOUT BALL)

Demonstrate the correct technique for approaching the ball using the two-step approach. Explain that the purpose of the approach is to allow the spiker to move quickly to the ball wherever it is set. The approach will also add velocity to the spike, but that is not the major purpose of the approach.

In the approach, start about 5 to 6 feet from where the spiker will contact the ball. Shorter players might start a little closer, taller ones a little further back.

Beginning position - Ready to move, muscles on stretch, weight slightly forward, arms pulled back, weight on right foot (for right-handers). As the ball is tossed, a right-handed spiker will step forward with the left foot, hopping off that foot as a sort of pre-hop, turning the body 45° in the air; in planting for the attack jump, place the feet well in front of the body, with the right foot hitting the floor just prior to the left foot. As the feet hit on the plant, the arms should already be in front of the body and swung directly overhead before the feet leave the ground. In this demonstration, pick one of the better performers and toss the ball around to different areas of the net, allowing the hitter to demonstrate how the approach is used to get to the ball. Ask the group to comment on why each spiking error occurred.

Demonstrate and walk the group through the approach, using three lines facing the net. Use the verbal cues to be certain the footwork is correct. Explain that everything is reversed for left-handers. Verbal cues: weight on right foot (left for left-handers), arms back, step with left, hop, turn 45°, plant feet well in front of body, freeze!

Figure 3 - Three-Line Approach, Pause and Hit Drill

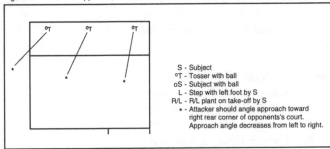

S - Subject
°T - Tosser with ball
oS - Subject with ball
L - Step with left foot by S
R/L - R/L plant on take-off by S
* - Attacker should angle approach toward
right rear corner of opponents's court.
Approach angle decreases from left to right.

TWO-STEP APPROACH, PAUSE, ATTACK A TWO BALL

Attacker should angle approach toward right rear corner of opponent's court. Approach angle decreases from left to right.

This drill combines the approach and spike, but adds a pause period, which allows the spiker to concentrate on footwork, plant for the jump and then correctly execute the jump and spike as in the previous drill (see Figure 3).

SUGGESTIONS

1. Prior to the approach, have the spiker start with the arms already back and keep them back during the approach. This simplifies the approach because the spiker does not have to think about armswing synchronization while concentrating on footwork.

2. On the footwork, use the following verbal cues.

a. Ready, arms back, weight on right foot (left foot for left-handers), angle approach toward right rear corner of opponent's court.

b. Step with free foot (left).

c. Left-foot plant, using a slight hop, push off and slightly turn, so body is 45° angle to the net upon R-L plant.

d. In planting to jump, land with feet spread shoulder width. The trailing foot will contact the floor a moment before the left foot. The arms remain extended behind the back until the attacker prepares to jump.

3. The approach, pause, toss and hit drill execution.

After the attacker pauses in the ready-to jump-and-spike position and before the tosser releases the ball for the spike, the spiker and tosser should both check during the pause position to be certain the spiker is 5 feet from the net (tosser is 4). The body is at a 45° angle to net, open to tosser, feet are spread shoulder width apart, legs are bent 110°, trunk is forward 45° and arms are still back, ready to thrust upward on release of ball by tosser. Attacker's eyes should be focused on the tosser. After making necessary adjustment, the tosser will toss the ball 4 feet higher than spiker's standing height, straight up in front of spiker's attack shoulder for spiker to swing arms upward, jump and hit with a high elbow, followed by a vigorous wrist snap.

SPIKING DRILL - COMBINING PROPER ARMSWING WITH THE TWO-STEP APPROACH AND THE TWO-BALL SPIKE

In this next drill, the structure is the same as in the previous drill. The only difference is no prolonged pause on the plant and a slightly higher toss. The tosser will release the ball as the spiker's left foot hits the ground.

The tosser must toss the ball straight up 6 feet higher than the attacker's head so it comes down 1 foot in front of the attacker's spiking shoulder.

The attacker should start with the arms extended backward. As the left step is taken, the arms remain back until the R-L plant. Spiker continues to plant within 1 foot of tosser and 5 feet from net.

I suggest a verbal cue walk-through with the entire group before adding the tossed ball to the sequence.

The verbal cues are as follows:

1. Medium ready position, weight on right foot, arms extended backward;
2. step with the left foot, taking a natural walking step, arms remain back; and
3. push off the left foot with a little hop and turn the body slightly to the right for a right-handed spiker (just the opposite for left-hander) and plant both feet at a 45° angle to the net. On the plant, the arms are swung upward and should be at the top of their upward arc, ready to lift the body off the ground as the leg's extensors drive the spiker off the ground to meet the descending ball.

From this basic teaching process, the beginner has learned to stress consistency and ball control, the importance of simplified double arm swing, the 45° approach and plant, the high spiking elbow, the aggressive wrist snap and the soft landing.

Most common errors are:

1. Toss incorrectly synchronized too low or high or not straight up and down.
2. Attacker approaching too slowly. Only the first step can be slow. The push off the left foot and the armswing, plant and jump must be very aggressive.
3. Spiker failing to drive up or running underneath the ball. The spiker must plant, with the feet in front of the body, a minimum of 1 foot behind the descending ball.
4. Late arms. Both arms must be overhead as the jumper leaves the ground.
5. Low elbow, non-aggressive wrist snap.

SUMMARY

The deep hit, low toss teaching method will result in efficient learning in the shortest period of time. As the basic technique is learned, advanced and more powerful techniques can be added. From this basic teaching process, the beginner has learned to stress consistency and ball control, the importance of simplified double armswing, the 45° approach and plant, the high spiking elbow, the aggressive wrist snap and the soft landing.

For later transfer purposes, this technique has already taught the hitter how to (1) hit the overpass (with no approach); (2) hit the two ball (combination play, second tempo shot); (3) hit from any distance from the net (back-row attack); and (4) how to hit a ball that has been approached too quickly (the pause and hit).

Spiking is not a difficult skill to learn if you simplify the process and allow step-by step success, but it must be a meaningful progression that blends into the proper execution of the skill in game conditions. This progression meets that requirement.

Don Shondell is the head men's volleyball coach at Ball State University in Muncie, Ind.

Recognizing and Correcting
Backwards Footwork in the Spike Approach

Recognizing and Correcting Backwards Footwork in the Spike Approach

DAVE ORREN

At the University of St. Thomas, we have a varsity and junior varsity. Each year, we keep a total of 20 players, about half of which are freshmen. About two or three freshmen each year will have backwards footwork. The St. Thomas coaches have coached at summer camps for high school players for many years. Except for the truly elite camps, about 25% to 35% of the players have backwards footwork.

It is very difficult to correct backwards footwork when it is ingrained. For years, we tried without success. At one point, we had concluded that it was all but impossible to correct backwards footwork — the "you cannot teach an old dog new tricks" theory. We had resigned ourselves to working to enhance players' backwards footwork in an effort to minimize the bad effects. We worked on transition to get players back further and more quickly so they could generate the necessary horizontal speed to maximize their vertical jump.

We worked on planting the heels simultaneously to minimize the inefficiency of a backwards heel plant in transferring horizontal speed into vertical jump. We were never completely comfortable with this, however. We wanted to have an excellent team and we knew that excellent teams have few, if any, players with backwards footwork. And, it was a matter of recognizing that in Division III, the diamonds you get are often in the rough and your only choice, if you want to reach your highest potential, is that you must polish them.

A few years ago, the St. Thomas coaching staff made the collective decision that we were going to concentrate on correct footwork and that no player with backwards footwork was going to be on the team as a sophomore. A player may have had backwards footwork the first year, but would learn correct footwork by the sophomore year. This article contains some of the things we learned along the way about putting this goal into practice.

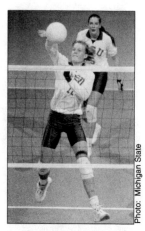

According to Orren, excellent teams have very few, if any, players with backwards footwork.

CORRECT FOOTWORK

The correct four-step approach for a right-handed hitter is Right-Left-RightLeft (R-L-RL). The first step begins the approach and generates some horizontal speed. The second step generates the majority of the horizontal speed and really amounts to a long leap forward, similar in some ways to the takeoff for a long jump. The last two steps occur almost simultaneously, with the hitter planting the heels and jumping. The heel plant converts the horizontal speed into vertical jump. The hitter's body should be slightly turned at the time of jumping so that the left shoulder is slightly closer to the net than the right shoulder and the left foot is slightly closer to the net than the right foot.

BACKWARDS FOOTWORK

Backwards footwork, at least with players we see at the college level, consists of the sequence L-R-LR or the sequence L-R-RL. The hitter with backwards footwork, just like the hitter with correct footwork, will turn

Photo: Ball State

Orren believes backwards footwork must be changed because the backwards sequence does not smoothly efficiently convert horizontal speed into vertical jump.

the body slightly at the time of jumping so that the left shoulder is slightly closer to the net than the right shoulder and the left foot is slightly closer to the net than the right foot.

ANALYZING FOOTWORK

Hitters are very consistent with their footwork. Most hitters will use either correct footwork almost all of the time. Very few players switch back and forth between the two types of footwork. You will only need to watch a player do 10 to 15 approaches to know for sure the type of footwork being used.

To analyze footwork, set up hitting lines with two or three players at a time and watch the players as they hit. This is the quickest and most efficient way to see whether a player has correct or backwards footwork. Trying to analyze footwork during games or in scrimmage situations does not work well because distractions abound. The ball is in the air, it is being dug, it is being set and by the time you look at the hitter, he/she is already in the air. Analyzing footwork by watching game tapes is also not very efficient because it takes an awful lot of time.

IT IS IMPORTANT TO CHANGE

After you have analyzed your players' footwork, you might wonder, "Why is it important to change backwards footwork? The players with backwards footwork hit some very impressive spikes and all hitters, even those with correct footwork, make mistakes. Sure backwards footwork is ugly, but is correcting it only a matter of aesthetics?" Be careful of these thoughts. They are rationalizations and the first signs of avoidance of the difficult task of correcting backwards footwork.

To analyze footwork, set up hitting lines with two or three players at a time and watch the players as they hit. This is the quickest and most efficient way to see whether a player has correct or backwards footwork.

Why is it important to change? As mentioned earlier, there are two types of backwards footwork sequences: L-R-LR and L-R-RL. Each has negative effects on the hitter's performance. The L-R-LR backwards sequence does not smoothly or efficiently convert horizontal speed into vertical jump. This is because the heel plant for the left foot (which is closer to the net) happens before the heel plant for the right foot (which is further from the net). The left-foot heel plant absorbs the forward speed instead of converting it into the vertical jump. The LR heel plant is not mechanically sound. (This article will not go into detail on the mechanics of this approach, but to get some feel for why this sequence is bad, walk four steps using the L-R-LR sequence; make sure that your third step is further ahead than your fourth step.) We estimate that the backwards sequence of L-R-LR reduces a player's jump by 10% to 20% compared to what it would be with correct footwork.

The backwards L-R-RL sequence has a smoother and more efficient heel plant than the backwards L-R-LR sequence. However, it does not generate as much horizontal speed as the correct R-L-RL sequence. This is because the second step is a skip step where the hitter both pushes off and lands with the right foot. This skip step does not generate any speed; it merely maintains whatever speed the player's approach has already generated. To generate the same amount of horizontal speed as in a correct approach, the player with backwards footwork must take an extra step at the beginning of the approach to generate the necessary horizontal speed. Therefore, a player with the L-R-RL backwards sequence needs a longer approach to hit successfully. This means that this player will hit well in warm-up and on serve receive, where there is adequate time to take a long approach. Transition hitting is another story, because the player often does not have time to get back far enough to use backwards footwork effectively. Backwards footwork also has a bigger effect on middle hitters than on outside hitters because the middle hitters have less time on transition.

Both types of backwards footwork sequences lead to other problems, as well. Because the second step is with the right foot, it is harder for the backwards footwork hitter to plant the feet with the shoulders and feet at an appropriate angle to the net. Backwards footwork hitters tend to face the net squarely. Consequently, the backwards footwork hitter has a harder time hitting cross-court from the left side and down the line from the right side.

With both types of backwards footwork, it is also harder to adjust to less-than-perfect sets because you have to commit to your approach earlier to get the necessary horizontal speed. Also, if your team runs quick plays or timing plays and your team has some players with correct footwork and some with backwards footwork, it makes it harder on the setter. The setter does not get the same cues from all of the hitters regarding when to set. A team that runs a quick offense is better off if its hitters all have the same type of footwork.

Another reason to change a player's footwork, and this is long-term, is that the player may someday become a coach. The better you teach your players now, the better it is going to be later on when these skills filter down to the next volleyball generation. You would not want his/her players to follow in their coach's backwards footsteps.

CHANGE IS DIFFICULT

There are many factors that make it difficult to change a player's footwork. Complicating this is the fact that correct footwork in spiking is an all-or-nothing proposition; you cannot be "just a little backwards" in your footwork and you cannot change footwork a little bit at a time.

Footwork and timing are two inseparable parts of the spike approach. You must, therefore, teach footwork and timing at the same time. You can do preliminary drills without the ball until you are blue in the face, but all this does is lay a very thin (albeit important) groundwork for teaching correct footwork. Because footwork and timing are intertwined, the player must approach, for the most part, at full speed. After you have

"Jumping is a fundamental aspect of volleyball that can often be overlooked during the evaluation of an athlete's overall attacking or blocking performance. As a coach, you may be more concerned with the tactics of team play or the arm swing or footwork patterns to be overly concerned with the more basic aspects of jumping technique. As a coach, it is natural to assume that your athletes are jumping and reaching as high as they possibly can. Regardless, I believe there is always potential for the athlete to improve jumping technique."

(Peter Vint. The mechanics of motion: scientific aspects of jumping. *Coaching Volleyball*, December/January 1994.)

Another reason to change a player's footwork, and this is long-term, is that the player may someday become a coach. The better you teach your players now, the better it is going to be later on when these skills filter down to the next volleyball generation.

According to Peter Vint, in his article titled "The Mechanics of Motion: Scientific Aspects of Jumping" (*Coaching Volleyball*, December/January 1994), "There are two fundamental mechanical concepts which need to be understood before [any coach can discuss] some of the more advanced aspects of jumping -- center of gravity and projectile motion. [CG will be discussed here.]

The center of gravity (CG) may be roughly thought of as the "balancing point" of an object (in our case, the object refers to the human body). The CG is the point at which all of the weight of the body is considered to act. The CG can also be considered to represent a single point which characterizes the general motion of the entire body. In humans (in a position with the arms at the sides), the CG lies at about 54-56% of standing height -- a position slightly below the navel.

completed the preliminary drills without the ball, there is no slow speed you can actually use to hit the ball. Compare this to the learning process for a basketball lay-up, in which a beginner can walk through and then gradually increase speed as coordination and skill are learned. Once the set is in the air, the player's focus is on the ball and all thoughts of footwork are gone. At this point, the player has no awareness of his/her footwork. Some automatic, deeply ingrained internal computer directs the movement of the feet without any conscious input from the player. A hitter's footwork, correct or backwards, is beyond immediate control. If players stop to think about their footwork after the set is in the air, they will be unable to get to the ball in time to hit it. Changing footwork is difficult because you have to reprogram this automatic, deeply ingrained internal computer. Until this re-programming becomes deeply ingrained, players will probably revert back to backwards footwork in game situations.

Motivation (or lack thereof) makes it difficult to change footwork because the player will get decidedly worse over the short term. Many players with backwards footwork can hit relatively well using it. Players' hitting will often get decidedly worse in the short term while they are learning correct footwork. Players will get frustrated when this happens and will want to quit working on their footwork. The coach's crucial role in motivating the player to continue to work at changing footwork is discussed later in this article.

CUEING THE APPROACH

The player who is learning correct footwork needs a cue or focus early in the approach to be in sync for using correct footwork. A workable cue at the second step of the four-step approach is for the player to put the left foot down consciously and to begin the long leap forward that is the correct second step. The player does not need to complete the correct second step consciously because the internal computer will take over at this point and automatically complete the correct approach. As a visual aid for the players, put a piece of tape on the floor about 8 feet from the net for the player to put the left foot on. As a visual aid for the coach, have the players put their left knee pads down at their ankles so you can more easily see that each player is correctly using his/her left foot for the second step in the approach.

This specific cue seems to be critical to reprogramming a player's footwork. Consciously placing the right foot down for the first step or consciously placing the left foot down for the second step does not work because a player with deeply ingrained backwards footwork will unconsciously insert an extra step and revert to backwards footwork. It is essential that the player consciously begin the correct second step before completing the approach on automatic.

You have to do a lot of work to get to the point where you can use this cue. You must spend a lot of time and effort using the early drill progressions in order to ingrain the correct footwork patterns. Teach not only the footwork, but also cue the footwork when doing the early drill progressions by slapping the ball to signal the players when to do the cue for their approach.

DRILLS

This drill progression is designed to first teach correct footwork and then to introduce timing. The first three drills involve no timing whatsoever — they are simply used to ingrain correct footwork. The remaining drills are designed to introduce timing a little bit at a time, but only after players master correct footwork.

For these drills, you will need a net and a bucket of balls. For the second and third drills, the coach may need a platform to stand on in order to hold a ball above the net. These drills are best done with five or fewer players per coach. The drill progression is as follows:

When using progressive drills to teach footwork, move slowly from one to the next. Give players a chance to ingrain what they have learned before moving on.

1. Footwork without a ball.
2. Footwork with a ball held in the way of the swing.
3. Footwork over a prone body with a ball held in the way of the swing. (Have one of the players lay down on the floor at about 6 feet from the net, between where the second and third steps occur. By stepping over this player while taking their approaches, the others will have to lengthen and speed up their second step.)
4. Footwork with a ball lifted in the way of the swing.
5. Footwork with a one toss.
6. Footwork with a two toss.
7. Footwork with a high, outside toss.
8. Footwork off of sets.
9. Footwork in game situations.

Progress slowly from one drill to the next. Give the players a chance to ingrain what they have learned before moving on to the next level in the progression. Ingrain it well enough that the players will not revert back to old habits when you go on to the next level. The coach must watch the players' approaches closely during drills to make sure that they are doing the correct footwork every time they approach. If the footwork breaks down, go back a progression or two.

Each time you begin a footwork session, start at the beginning of the drill progression. As your players get more proficient at a certain level, you can spend less time reviewing it, but it is important that you constantly go back to the very basics if you want to ingrain correct footwork. This constant repetition and review is an excellent way to make correct footwork automatic during game situations.

Players need constant feedback during the drills. Encourage them when they do the footwork correctly. Stop them immediately when they use backwards footwork. In fact, in drills 2-6, watch to see that the players use the correct cue to start their approach. If a player does not put the left foot down on the tape and correctly begin the second step, pull the ball back and do not let the player hit it. Then immediately have the hitter do the approach correctly. Early on in drills, the coach is the one who must give the constant feedback. Teach players to work with each other and to give necessary feedback to each other so that eventually they can work on their own.

If you coach younger players, you probably also get footwork that is actually no footwork at all — just a stutter step. The player kind of dances up to the net, stops and then jumps to hit. This drill progression may also help a player with a stutter-step approach.

> *If you coach younger players, you probably also get footwork that is actually no footwork at all -- just a stutter step. The player kind of dances up to the net, stops and then jumps to hit. This drill progression may also help a player with a stutter-step approach.*

FREQUENCY

How often do you work on changing backwards footwork? During our preseason at St. Thomas, a coach will spend about 30 minutes each day with our backwards footwork club, or Club Foot Backwards, as they have come to call themselves. After the regular season starts, the players need to do something every day—perhaps as part of their warm-up routine or after practice. It is important for the coach to work with the group of players periodically to monitor their progress and to show them that correct footwork is important to the coaches.

What are the pros and cons of correcting backwards footwork during the season? If you correct footwork during the season, the player's hitting effectiveness will be greatly reduced for a month or more. If you do not correct footwork during the season, it will not get done. It is almost impossible for players to correct footwork by themselves. A coach needs to work directly and intensively with a player and to give immediate feedback in order for any meaningful progress to be made. Unless you can work extensively with your players in the off-season, it is a now or never proposition. For players on developmental teams, it is an obvious choice to correct the footwork during the season. If one of your important varsity players has backwards footwork, you have a dilemma. There may be some middle ground where you can teach the player enough of the drills during the season to work on them during the off-season and yet not push the drills so much that it has a negative effect on hitting during the season.

How long does it take to make the change? We introduce footwork drills during the preseason and continue during the season. For some players, this is enough. For most players, however, this only lays the groundwork. These players need to work diligently on footwork in the off-season in order to make the change.

MOTIVATION AND COMMITMENT

The coach must provide motivation to change. Every year, we tell our players with backwards footwork that we expect them to learn correct footwork by this time next year. We let them know that it can be done by telling them that there have been many players like them in past years who have made the change. And we point out prominent examples of success stories among the sophomores, juniors and seniors.

The coach must provide permission to change. A player will make many hitting mistakes while learning correct footwork. This will affect confidence and possibly playing time. When players make hitting mistakes—and they will—you have to be supportive. Basically, you have to give them permission to make mistakes in order to change their footwork. There is, no doubt, a limit to the number of mistakes you can accept, but you need to make some allowances for each player. Without that, all of your talk is meaningless.

Also, each player must make a commitment to change. Of necessity, the coach must teach the drills for correct footwork over the course of the season. Players need to learn the drills and progressions well enough to do them on their own. A player must make a commitment to follow through and do the necessary work and suffer through the period when spiking gets worse. The player must also make a commitment to work alone through the off-season when the coach is not there to work with or provide encouragement. Certainly, part of the player's commitment comes from knowing the coach feels correct footwork is important and that all of the efforts are appreciated. However, a bigger part of the commitment must come from inside the player who wants to compete at the highest level.

Dave Orren is the head women's volleyball coach at the University of St. Thomas in St. Paul, Minn.

Position Specific Drilling

Position Specific Drilling

LISA LOVE

In volleyball, position specific drilling concentrates on one thing — cultivating a need. A coach must know exactly what skills need to be honed on a day-to-day basis, what the objective of the practice is and what is the best way to go about grooming players for certain positions.

For the purposes of this article, concentration will be on three positions on the court — the setter, outside hitter and middle blocker. Examples of isolated drilling opportunities regarding those three positions will be provided.

At USC, to communicate what is expected from each of those three positions, we provide each of our athletes a job description at the beginning of the season, with reminders during the year.

The middle blocker's No. 1 duty is to block balls or deny court.

Photo: University of Southern California

SETTING

The needs of the setter position are varied. For the most part, we want the setter to have great location, to make proper decisions and to provide floor leadership. In essence, the setter is the true center of the action.

OUTSIDE HITTING

Ordinarily, coaches differentiate between opposites and swing hitters, but for the purpose of this article, both positions will be combined.

To begin, an outside hitter must pass very effectively, between a 2.2 and a 2.4 percentage rating. (A 3.0 percentage rating means all three hitters can be set; 1.0 means only one hitter can be set due to the pass.)

The last thing the outside hitter wants to do is make a hitting error. Therefore, we do not want our outside hitters to be intimidated by the block.

In addition, we need for them to hit very efficiently; an outside hitter is going to swing more than anyone else on the court, by the nature of the position. An outside hitter must hit very efficiently, with these priorities in mind: 1) the first objective is to kill the ball; 2) the second objective is to hit a ball effectively. Perhaps it is blocked or dug, but either way, that is acceptable; 3) the last thing the outside hitter wants to do is to make a hitting error. Therefore, we do not want our outside hitters to be intimidated by the block. That is one of the most difficult concepts to teach an outside hitter. It is the role of the hitter coverage — to protect the area around the hitter -- if they are blocked.

MIDDLE BLOCKING

The middle blocker's No. 1 duty is to block balls or deny court. The best way to impact a match is by blocking balls or having a profound blocking presence. A middle blocker is not good simply as a quick hitter; however, a middle blocker is very good as a great middle blocker with marginal hitting ability. That is how that person will have the greatest impact for the team.

The second objective of the middle blocker is to be available to hit a first tempo or quick set. At USC, we utilize a quick attack in our offense. We want our middle blocker to be available to hit all of those quicks.

Love believes the outside hitter must not be intimidated by the block; the hitter coverage is there to protect the area around the hitter if they are blocked.

Mark Pavlik, in his article titled "Setter and Quick Hitter Efficiency" (*Coaching Volleyball*, December/January 1991), states that getting the hitter and setter in sync is fairly easy.

"Begin with establishing where at the net the setter will penetrate. I prefer to have the setter penetrate to the right front corner then move to the pass at target. This enables the setter to view the entire court and have the weight forward when setting. This should also eliminate any back-pedaling to balls passed to the extreme right of the court.

Secondly, insist the setter jumpset the ball at every opportunity. This promotes a quicker exchange from setter to hitter. Show where the ball is to be set when running any quick series (i.e. 31, 41, 51, 61, etc.). The preference is to set the ball anywhere from the midline of the setter's body to the left shoulder in relation to the net."

Availability is the key word. The middle blocker must transition attack from all sorts of positions along the net; the approach patterns are more horizontal and less vertical, so they must master those footwork patterns and therein be available to hit all of the time.

Finally, a middle blocker must be relentlessly aggressive. A player in this position cannot stop — they have got to be the warrior or the player on the floor who provides the controlled aggression throughout the entire match.

EMOTIONAL STYLE

The way players conduct themselves on the court is crucial. A coach must look for a relentlessly aggressive middle blocker who can block and hit well — or instill those traits in current players. In addition, a coach must have a controlled, dynamic outside hitter who can pass and hit well. Finally, a coach must have a setter who sets the ball well, makes great decisions and provides leadership. Technical skills are not enough; the right personality and a penchant for leadership in a particular position are also crucial elements.

In creating the types of drills to exercise those particular three positions, it is important for players to perform at a high level in practice. Practice serves only to provide a foundation for match performance. Therefore, a coach is always looking at match feedback — how well does this player play in a match? Is she actually doing what she has been rehearsing? A player may or may not change behavior during a match; our goal is to provide a comfort level where players perform on an even keel most of the time.

Players may start slowly and finish strong; players may start strong and the score reaches 16-16 and they start tipping instead of hitting the ball. Players may be solid in passing, yet when the score gets tight, their eyes get big.

Players change, so as we work to isolate positions and drill them on the court, we are evaluating match conditions. We segment the match — the beginning, the midpoint and the end of the match. Feedback from matches provides us with purpose when drilling by position.

DRILL DEVELOPMENT

In preparing to develop drills, the first thing I would suggest is to be creative. I am going to share with you some of the things we do with setters, middle blockers and outside hitters on an isolated court. But first, let us consider drilling in general.

Obviously, we are going to drill to strengthen our weaknesses, as well as to enhance our strengths and to address the needs I mentioned above. Our drills had better be challenging, game-like, organized and effective. Otherwise, they are a waste of everyone's time. If we want a player to be good at 16-16, then we need to create a drill environment that allows for that opportunity on a regular basis. We also want to make sure that the outside hitter, middle blocker and setter have regular opportunities to prac-

Photo: Bob Kalmbach

tice what they do correctly. Indeed, that is a mental thing — it is as much about training confidence as it is technical expertise. Do not forget to do what you do right. Remember, players change. A coach is trying to get an athlete to be the same in all situations.

One of the ways we go about this is to use more than one court in a practice setting. We will set up two to four courts for the most effective and efficient practice gym. We may have the outside hitters working on one court, the middles on another court, setters on another court. Or we may incorporate a small group: working one middle blocker, a setter, an outside hitter on one court;

Players change, so as we work to isolate positions and drill them on the court, we are evaluating match conditions. We segment the match -- the beginning, the midpoint and the end of the match. Feedback from matches provides us with purpose when drilling by position.

one middle, a setter, an outside hitter on another court; or maybe three backcourt players training on another court. Use of multiple courts will help you with practice effectiveness.

Do not be afraid to break your team apart and practice under isolated circumstances. Each player has a role or must maintain 1/6 of the effort of the group. There is no denying that any one, two or three of your players has to perform in that position under isolated circumstances very often in a match.

ISOLATED SITUATIONS APPLIED

For example, in a game situation, Team B is against Team A; Team B knows very well that Sue Smith is a 2.4 passer and the other passer is less proficient. Who is going to receive most of the serves? Who is going to be isolated by the opponents and worked during the course of the match? How well the targeted passer manages receiving 2/3 to 3/4 of all of the served balls is key to your team having success. Therefore, if you do not practice her in those isolated circumstances, she is going to have a hard time managing that in a match.

Another example of being isolated is the exploitation of the short blocker. Chances are, opponents will consistently attack over the short blockers. That blocker must work well under those circumstances and remain efficient, therein allowing the floor defense to be effective.

Being isolated in a match yet still being a part of the team goes hand in hand. A third example is isolation generated from within. Imagine you have a team that has one particularly strong outside hitter. Who is the setter going to set seven out of 10 balls to? The entire audience knows she is going to set the ball to Carrie Crunch. It is Carrie Crunch against the world. Carrie Crunch has to practice in the gym against six or seven defenders in a predictable offensive environment. By the nature of a single dimensional offense, she is going to hit; the defense will be prepared and she responds accordingly.

Those are just some examples of why it is good to take your team apart and practice them well in their positions, not just for the technical aspects, but also for the match dynamics. The technical side of it is pretty easy, but the match dynamics are a little bit more sophisticated. How

Love believes players must play strong throughout the match; they cannot start tipping just because the score reaches 16-16.

well those players manage that accountability in a certain position is how well your team will function together as six.

Following are a few position specific drills to impact individual players.

BASIC SETTER PRESSURE DRILL

The setter goes to the setting position; the balls are in the ball cart in position six (center back). The hitters form a hitting line. The coach places the hitters in a numerical order. Spread the hitters randomly so that they approach their set from a variety of positions while remaining in the assigned numerical order. The coach is going to give the setter tosses as quickly as possible.

The goal of this drill is for the hitters to score a consecutive number of kills as determined by the coach.

(During the drill, tosses may vary in quality and pace, therein stressing the setter as deemed appropriate by the coach. The setter is practicing leadership, decision making and match management under stress.)

Remember one thing — explain the parameters of the drill for the setter: Give her the goal and let her do the drill. Your setter is going to get frazzled, frustrated and may have trouble getting out of the drill. That does not have to be a negative! Coach the setter privately and let her know that she is developing her court presence under these conditions just as much as her ability to deliver a nice set. If the drill does not become stressful, it is not indicative of the conditions of the match at times. That feedback is important, especially when her frustration level is high.

If you have setter competition (more than one setter you are evaluating), you simply must structure the drill a bit differently. Make a passing line from zone five (left back) and have setters penetrate from zone one (right back) alternately.

Your setter is going to get frazzled, frustrated and may have trouble getting out of the drill. That does not have to be a negative! Coach the setter privately and let her know that she is developing her court presence under these conditions just as much as her ability to deliver a nice set.

To begin the drill, the coach serves the ball to the passer, who passes and calls the set; the setter takes it from there. The goal of each setter is to get a certain number of consecutive kills before her partner. The drill is most realistic off of a passed ball.

TWO VS. SIX DRILL

For the two vs. six drill, the hitter can hit anything from anywhere, but to get one big point the hitter must consecutively kill three balls. The hitter's goal is to get six big points before the defense earns 25 denials. (Have a flip scorer to help keep score for both sides.)

(If you run this drill using rally scoring, my best guess is this is a bad choice. The inherent challenge of the drill did not happen. The hitter will win decisively. The team with possession of the ball, even though the offense is predictable, usually has a decisive advantage.)

To vary the drill, add another hitter, utilizing the same format. The speed with which the coach runs the drill will put more pressure on the setter and the passer. In addition, the type of ball served can then create the type of circumstances that you want. (Another option is just a basic outside hitter sequence.)

If I were reviewing a practice plan for an outside hitter sequence, it might read PHBHDHB. This translates into a drill where an outside hitter, working with a setter, must successfully execute consecutive touches on the ball — a Pass, Hit, Block, Hit, Dig, Hit and Block, to complete the drill. The drill is initiated with a serve. From that point, all executions are initiated either by coaches on platforms or by live attackers hitting a designated zone. If the hitter misses any part of the sequence, the hitter must start over. The next criteria that can be placed on the hitter is to vary her attacking zones on the net.

QUICK VS. QUICK

Finally, for the middles, we often utilize an exchange drill that we title Quick vs. Quick. It is ordinarily done with a full backcourt defense on each side of the net supporting the defensive efforts of a middle blocker. The only front-row players are the setter and the middle blocker.

The scoring format is rally score to five. The only way a point can be scored is by a kill or stuff block by the middle blockers. No points are awarded on a violation; however, the team not in violation earns possession of the ball. Ordinarily, a coach alternates initiating play to each team. Any poor pass limiting the setter's ability to set the quick would result in a backcourt attack. Although a point cannot be scored by a backcourt attacker, a kill would result in an earned possession of the ball.

Set up more than one net in practice and isolate by positions, working the drill as game-like as possible. The better your individual players are in their singular positions, the better they will be in a group.

Lisa Love is the head women's volleyball coach at the University of Southern California.

Section V: The Block

Blocking: The Key to Volleyball Success

Blocking: The Key to Volleyball Success

DON SHONDELL

The spike's velocity and the attacker's closeness to the blocker make blocking unquestionably the quickest skill in volleyball. Strong blocking is a requirement for success, especially in men's volleyball, where speed makes balls hit into the gap between players virtually impossible to dig. The blocker's responsibility—if he/she cannot "roof" the ball for a quick score or side-out—is to channel the ball to the digger or deflect it to a teammate.

Mental and physical preparation are crucial elements in the skill of blocking.

THE PSYCHOLOGICAL ASPECT OF BLOCKING

Blocking success can be measured in various ways, but perhaps most important is the psychological intimidation of the opponent. Intimidated attackers often hit out or resort to the tip to avoid being blocked. An aggressive attacker's whole game can be destroyed through the embarrassment of having several balls blocked in the face.

THE SKILL OF BLOCKING

Mental preparation. Limited time makes the blocker's preliminary preparation for actual contact vital. The blocker must deal with many variables, some out of his/her control; players must use what they know about opponents to set up correctly prior to the attack. Blockers can be alerted through scouting reports to opponents' tendencies by rotation, setters' habits and preferred plays and routes run by the attackers. Shot charts can inform them about hitters' shots in specific circumstances. For example: "Deep set— attacker hits to 5-zone corner. Tight set inside antenna— attacker normally hits line or outside wipe-off shot. Medium-depth set outside antenna— attacker hits sharp crosscourt." Such information helps blockers position themselves properly to stop attackers' preferred shots.

Physical preparation. The blocker should start with hands about head high, elbows in and pointing forward, palms facing the net, hands at a 45° angle to the floor and fingers spread. Hands are firm. He/she starts as close to the net as possible while allowing a vertical raise of the arms without touching the net.

For the blocker to be able to adjust to where the ball is hit, the legs should be slightly flexed and a rapid stutter step used to overcome inertia and to speed the adjustment. This is especially important when "read" blocking in the middle and when a quick move must be made to block a second option on a combination play. A player block in the middle in a read-block situation must also extend the arms almost completely before reading the setter's delivery. This results in jumping only with the legs, but should give the blocker enough height above the net to prevent a straight-down, undiggable hit. The blocker's extended arms will put the hands over the net more quickly as he/she reads the quick set. In blocking one-on-one, players should spread the arms slightly wider than in team blocking, because skilled middle attackers will cut the ball to either side of the single blocker.

After mental and physical preparation, the blocker is now ready to

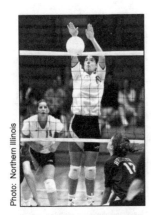

According to Shondell, blocking success can be measured in various ways, but perhaps most important is the psychological intimidation of the opponent.

execute the block with an excellent chance of success.

THE READ

In the read, the blocker watches the attackers out of the corner of the eye while concentrating on the setter, clueing in on where and at what speed and height the ball will be delivered. As the ball is passed to the setter, some setting options may be eliminated while others become more obvious. The blocker must adjust initially with the pass and again as the ball is set. Watching the setter, the blocker must be ready to tell team-mates if the attacker is moving inside or swinging to the opposite zone (where he/she must be picked up by another blocker if the blocking team is using a zone defense). In a match-up defense, the blocker stays with the assigned hitter by sliding behind the adjacent blocker. However, if the assigned attacker is hitting a one set, the blocker assigned to the quick hitter should slide in front of the adjacent blocker.

THE BLOCK

If the ball is set quickly, the blocker must try to block the attacker's preferred angle. A blocker's right hand should be against the spiking hand of a right-handed power angle hitter. Cut-back hitters should be blocked straight on, with a blocker's right hand slightly to the right side to cut off the sharp angle hit.

The blocker knows when to jump according to how deep the set is from the net and how hard the attacker hits the ball. Jumping too quickly sacrifices aggressiveness and the element of surprise. Generally, on balls hit deeper than 30 inches off the net, the hitter should contact the ball before the blocker extends the arms across the net. On sets closer than 30 inches, the blocker must commit earlier. If the set is on the net, the blocker surrounds the ball with the hands at virtually the same time as it is contacted by the attacker. (Note: The rules state that if the ball is completely on the attacker's side of the net, the attacker must touch the ball before the blocker. However, simultaneous contact is seldom called.)

When starting the blocking arm action, the blocker must be aware of the ball's velocity and its depth and angle in relation to the net. Ideally, the blocker either intercepts and rebounds the ball into the opponent's midcourt (preferably in front of the 3-meter line) or deflects it into his/her own backcourt in a controlled manner, enabling it to be set and attacked.

The blocker must be aware of the position of the body, arms and hands as he/she rebounds the ball. (Practicing the blocking arm action in front of a mirror and analyzing the arm and hand position is helpful.)

According to Newton's third law of physics, a force contacting a body suspended in air will result in an equal and opposite reaction by another part of the body. The lack of a spiking action is often what drives the blocker's body into the net.

The arms should rapidly and directly penetrate the net. The hands should be firm with the fingers spread to improve ball control and provide the greatest blocking surface. Just before contacting the ball the blocker should pike the hips, shrug the shoulders and tense the hands. Each helps to stabilize the airborne body and provide a force counter to the hard-driven volleyball. According to Newton's third law of physics, a force contact-ing a body suspended in air will result in an equal and opposite reaction by another part of the body. The lack of a spiking action is often what drives the blocker's body into the net.

THE REBOUND

The outside blocker should always finish the block (the ball contact) with palms facing the middle of the opponent's court. The middle blocker moving over to assist with the block is working a greater distance from the sideline and needs only to have shoulders square to the net to block the ball into the opponent's court. If he/she is arriving late, he/she should reach out with the lead hand to close the hole into which the hitter will probably try to direct the ball. The caution here is to be certain that shoulders remain parallel to the net and that the lead hand is in position to rebound the ball into the court.

SETTING THE BLOCK

In a one-on-one blocking situation, the attacker will probably try to cut the ball to the inside of the court, so the blocker should close into the court as the ball is hit and block with the arms spread wider than the shoulders. Blockers should set up inside and try to force the attacker to cut the ball back toward the near sideline digger.

In an outside team blocking situation, the outside blocker should set up directly in line with the blocker's approach angle to encourage the crosscourt spike. Just before the attacker's contact, the outside blocker must close toward the middle blocker. In a team block, the outside blocker should block with arms straight up, hands pointing at a 45° angle and thumbs about 4 inches apart. A good outside blocker will always turn the hands inward to block the ball into the attacker's midcourt while working outside in. The blocker must not reach outside the body line to block a line shot; that often sends the ball out of bounds. If the attacker's line shot is obvious and the blocker can move the entire body over and block in an inward direction, that is acceptable.

If the ball is deflected into the air in the blocker's backcourt, the blockers should look up to be certain the ball is not coming down on their heads. If the ball has not been deflected up, the blocker should step and turn in toward the backcourt player who should be digging the ball. As he/she turns, he/she moves off the net, ready to dig the ball if it is dug back. If it goes in another direction, he/she prepares for the transition responsibility, either setting or hitting. He/she moves off the net immediately after blocking, always toward midcourt.

When time permits, the middle blocker should use the slide step to move outside to block. This player should have shoulders square to the net and plant the inside foot close to the outside hitter. On the crosscourt hit, he/she should block with arms about 1 1/2 feet apart and hands at ball level. He/she must penetrate immediately to cut down the attacker's crosscourt angle. The importance of middle penetration is illustrated by the fact that 1 inch of penetration takes away about 7 1/2 inches of court at the crosscourt sidelines (so 12 inches of penetration will cut off 7 1/2 feet

Greg Giovanazzi, in his article titled "Blocking at the Collegiate Level" (1993), states: "Confidence, for some people is an innate quality; for most others, it must be learned. As a coach, you can design drills that will give players immediate satisfaction. Blocking is an area where you can offer athletes immediate success the first day; once they have success, they can start to think of themselves as good blockers.

Of course, it is important that when you give feedback in blocking it is positive and aggressive. Things like "Go after the ball," "Get the ball on their side," and "Grab the ball" are the kinds of verbal feedback that will pay a dividend because blocking is an aggressive skill."

From *Coaching Volleyball*, April/May 1993.)

Dave Shondell, in his article titled "Small High Schools Can Win With a Two-Blocker System" (*Coaching Volleyball*, June/July 1988), states that defensing the fast offense (which is seldom done effectively at the high school level) is an intense situation.

"When all three of the opponent's hitters are eligible, the team that uses the two-blocker system will have to give something up. In most cases, two blockers cannot effectively block all three hitters, so the coach must determine which hitter to ignore. If the opponent has a powerful left-side hitter, then the coach may decide to start the middle blocker on the opponent's left-side hitter and start the left-side player in front of the opponent's middle attacker, taking a chance with the right-side player hitter on an open net. If the opponent's middle game is suspect, then the coach may start the left-side player on the opponent's right-side hitter and the middle blocker on the opponent's left-side hitter, hoping the opponent can effectively run a fast offense in the middle.

of court sideline).

PLACING HANDS ON THE BALL

Players blocking at the same height helps guarantee an even block. If the center blocker reaches 24 inches above the net and the outside blocker only 12, hitters can find a weak seam between them. The blockers' hands should be at the height of the attacker's hitting hand; this assures an even "hand seam." Blockers should strive for penetration with palms at ball height and block the ball with the hands.

MIDDLE BLOCKER FOOTWORK

The middle blocker, when forced to move 20 feet quickly, should push off with the foot opposite the direction he/she wishes to move, stride out as far as possible with the lead foot, take one or two additional steps and then square away on the final plant with both feet pointing toward the net and hips touching the hips of the outside blocker.

COVERING THE TIPS

Blocker responsibilities for playing tips depend on the team's defensive system. In a 2-4 player back defense, the blockers, unless called off by a digger, should play a tip coming down within 8 feet of the block. The key in playing the tip or deflection is to turn as soon as the tip is read, take a step with the lead leg toward the ball and flex both legs, enabling the blocker to drop low to the ground. The blocker tries to bump the ball high in the vicinity of the 3-meter line to give all players enough time to spread out and run the transition offense. As a rule, if no one behind the blocker calls for the tip, he/she should go for it. Once an up-player starts for the ball, he/she is committed to play it.

SUMMARY

The major emphasis in blocking is mental and physical preparation, allowing the player to get in the best position to execute the actual block. Main features of the block are aggressiveness, direct penetration and a properly angled rebound. The blocker should penetrate the net immediately with properly shaped hands and either rebound the ball into the opponent's midcourt, deflect it into his/her own backcourt or force the spiker into an attack error.

An effective block is unquestionably the keystone of a successful defense. Because of its importance, much of a successful team's practice time is devoted to sharpening individual and team blocking skills.

Don Shondell is the head men's volleyball coach at Ball State University in Muncie, Ind.

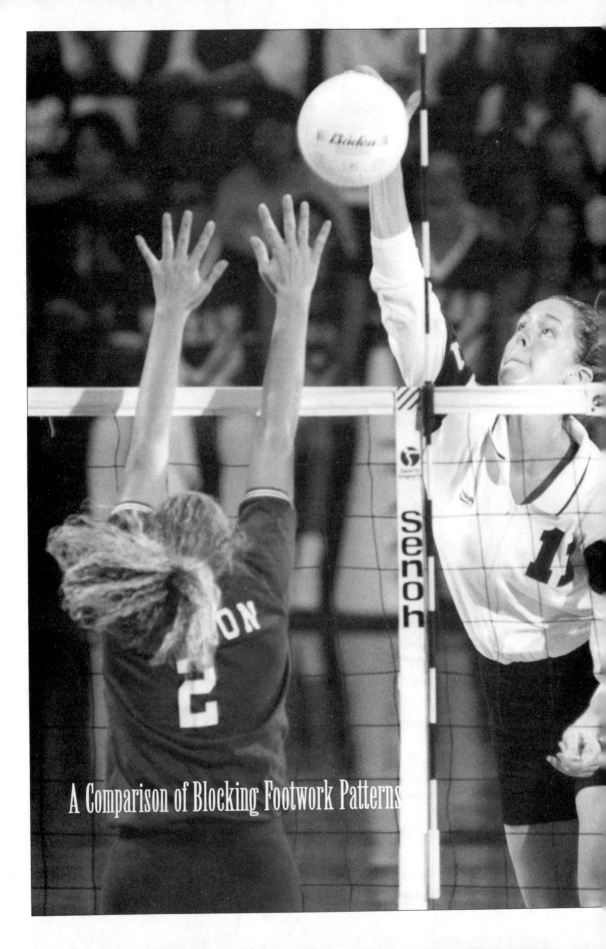

A Comparison of Blocking Footwork Patterns

A Comparison of Blocking Footwork Patterns

MASHALLAH FAROKHMANESH
AND CARL MCGOWN

The game of volleyball, like many others, has changed a great deal since its beginnings. Some of the greatest changes have been in blocking. Prior to the 1964 Olympic Games, reaching over the net to block was illegal and blocking was primarily defensive and not strongly related to team success. But by the 1974 World Games, a team's blocking average correlated higher with tournament rank, win-loss ratio and percentage of games won than any other factor. In the 1984 Olympic Games, blocking was second only to spiking in determining team success.

The middle blocker is probably the most important position. Middle blockers have more responsibility than others because they must block all of the quick middle sets, as well as the high outside sets. Typically, a middle blocker is a little taller and must jump a little higher than the outside blocker. The final match of the 1976 Olympic Games whereby Tomasz Wojtowicz of Poland almost single-handedly defeated the Soviet Union, is a good example of how a middle blocker can dominate a game.

According to the authors, the middle blocker position is crucial to an effective defense.

One of the middle blocker's most important tasks is to defend against volleyball's most common set: high to the sideline. To block outside, the middle blocker must move quickly along the net and coordinate with the end blocker to form an effective two-player block. The middle blocker can use many footwork patterns to move to the outside, but the slide step, the crossover step and the jab step are the most common.

SLIDE STEP

The slide step (see Figure 1) involves moving the lead foot laterally and closing the trailing foot to within 6 inches of the lead foot. The movement is repeated until jumping position is reached. Movement to the left is initiated by a lateral step to the left. This is followed by a quick slide step with the right foot, closing the gap to 6 inches again.

CROSS-OVER STEP

In the cross-over step (see Figure 2) the player crosses one foot in front of the other and begins to move parallel to the net (with running steps, if necessary) in the direction that the initial step was taken. If moving to the left, the player initiates with the right foot. From a stationary position, the right foot is crossed over the left; the next step is made with the left foot parallel to and in the same direction as the right.

JAB STEP

The jab step (see Figure 3) is executed by pivoting on the ball of one foot and taking a short step with the other. For a jab step to the left, for example, the blocker pivots on the ball of the right foot and takes the short step with the left foot. This is followed by a cross-over step with the right foot and movement continues to the left along the net.

MOST EFFECTIVE?

Various studies have attempted to determine which of the footwork

98

The authors recommend that coaches let blockers vary their footwork patterns according to individual preferences.

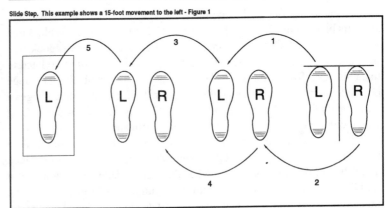

Slide Step. This example shows a 15-foot movement to the left - Figure 1

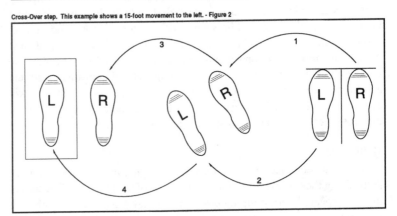

Cross-Over step. This example shows a 15-foot movement to the left. - Figure 2

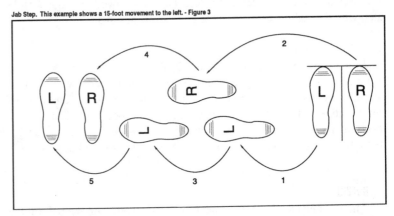

Jab Step. This example shows a 15-foot movement to the left. - Figure 3

patterns is fastest, but the findings conflict. Neither have they determined which footwork pattern leads to the most effective (fastest and highest) jump. A problem in every study was the use of only one starting position and distance, although blocking must be performed from many different spots along the net. Furthermore, most studies used experienced male players with established habits that may have affected the results. To examine more completely which technique is most effective for blocking, we conducted a study at Brigham Young University with both men and women in a beginning volleyball class, using two distances (9 and 15 feet) and measuring both movement time and vertical jump.

We chose the distances of 9 and 15 feet because a middle blocker is not always in the center of the court. When starting to block, the middle blocker must stay with the setter and middle hitter so that if the setter sets quickly to the middle, the middle blocker is ready to defend against the play. From any position in this middle area, the middle blocker must also be prepared to defend against the high outside attack.

We measured vertical jump because it is often more important than quickness. If the opposing team is unable to run a middle attack due to an errant pass, the middle blocker has ample time to move to the outside to execute the block. In this situation, the ability to jump high and penetrate the net is crucial. Even in situations that require the middle blocker to move quickly, vertical jump is still a prime consideration for a successful block.

In performing the three-step techniques, players took the following numbers of steps: slide step (five steps to cover 15 feet and three steps to cover 9 feet); cross-over step (four steps to cover 15 feet and three steps to cover 9 feet); and jab step (five steps to cover 15 feet and three steps to cover 9 feet).

STUDY RESULTS

We found little difference in speed among the footwork patterns (see Figure 4). This is true whether the middle blocker is a man or a woman, has to go left or right or must travel a short or long distance. The difference in movement time was only 0.0014 seconds between the fastest and slowest patterns. The jab step did produce the best vertical jump, but its advantage was just 0.6 inches, which is not a lot in volleyball. Given such minimal differences, we recommend that coaches let blockers vary their footwork patterns according to individual preference. If a coach wants to train all players with a specific style, we recommend the jab step because of its slight advantage over the other two techniques in speed and vertical jump.

Figure 4

Movement Direction	Movement Time (msec.)			Vertical Jump (inches)		
	Slide step	X-over step	Jab step	Slide step	X-over step	Jab step
9 ft. left	1610	1608	1606	17.6	17.5	17.8
15 ft. left	2084	2060	2064	17.6	17.7	18.0
9 ft. right	1636	1612	1595	17.7	17.7	18.9
15 ft. right	2050	2056	2060	17.8	17.8	18.2
Mean	1845	1834	1831	17.6	17.6	18.2

Mashallah Farokhmanesh is the assistant women's volleyball coach at Washington State University in Pullman, Wash. Carl McGown is the head men's volleyball coach at Brigham Young University in Provo, Utah., and is a USA Volleyball CAP certified coach.

Blocking and How to Read the Hitter

Blocking and How to Read the Hitter

CATHY GEORGE

A team's block is its first line of defense, its aggressive and explosive movement designed to shut down the opponent's offense. The significance of the block to a team's defense cannot be stressed enough, especially at the collegiate level. Essentially, if a team's blocking scheme breaks down, so does its defense.

While blocking is one of the more important skills in volleyball, it continues to be one of the most difficult skills for coaches to teach and players to understand. How many times have you watched your athletes try to overexecute the block, getting high over the net instead of crossing the net, only to get used by an opposing attacker? Or they misread the attacker and continually get beaten down the line or with a cut shot? These miscues are common, especially for the inexperienced player who tries to make blocking more complex than what is really needs to be.

The key to a good blocking team is to simplify the overall movement by reading all the cues. So instead of reacting to the situation, your players can anticipate the situation. This successful ability to read the cues comes with experience. This article will address effective training techniques that coaches may utilize in practice to develop a player's ability to read the opponent's attack and become a better blocker.

Photo: North Dakota State

While blocking is one of the most important skills in volleyball, it continues to be one of the most difficult skills for coaches to teach and players to master.

BLOCKING SCHEME

At some institutions, coaches do not have the type of player who has the overall physical ability to stuff block on a consistent basis. Instead, a coach must choose the block to channel the opponent's attack to the defensive players. Therefore, emphasize the establishment of a solid double block, forcing the opponent's hitters to work around it.

> The key to a good blocking team is to simplify the overall movement by reading all the cues.

Obviously, the first step in good blocking is correctly executing the skill, including foot movement and body placement. As a quick review, I have listed certain skill progression cues when executing proper blocking form.

Ready Position
- ○ Feet are shoulder width apart.
- ○ Toes are slightly inward with the weight on the balls of feet.
- ○ Knees are flexed about 20 degrees.
- ○ Arms with hands held high and ball-width apart.

Jump Takeoff and Lateral Movement
- ○ Knees bend to 80-90 percent on a high set; less bend when blocking a quick middle attack. It is possible to block or slow the ball down on a middle attack with half a jump.
- ○ On takeoff, arms should penetrate the net to intercept the ball before its crosses the plane of the net. I used to tell my players to go over the net, but they interpreted that as needing the arms to go above the net and balls were hitting down in front of them. Today, I tell them to press across the net so there is no confusion in the translation.

The inexperienced blocker all-too-often focuses on the speed of the ball instead of the movement of the attacker.

○ Shoulders should be shrugged and the stomach tightened just before contact to strengthen block.

○ Chin is tucked. This keeps your shoulders and arms forward.

○ On contact, see yourself block the ball.

○ On contact, there is no need to use any wrist action unless the attack is an offspeed shot. Outside blockers should press the block into the court.

○ Keep your hands in front of the ball so you can see your hands contact the ball. Good blockers see themselves block or touch every ball.

In terms of lateral movement, players should either use a side shuffle movement or an open, run and close movement. For covering short distances, the side shuffle is the preferred choice rather than the "open, run and close" method of blocking. On longer distances, the middle blocker may need to turn and run in order to get there in time.

EYE CONTACT PROGRESSION

Developing a player's eye contact ability is the most difficult blocking skill to teach. The inexperienced athlete all too often will focus on the speed of the ball instead of the movement of the attacker. Also, a young player does not communicate where the attackers are going and then is not ready to intercept the attack.

How do you develop good eye contact? The following three steps are suggestions to increase this development. Blockers must focus on the serve receive pass. Is it off the net or directly to the setter? Can the opponent run a combination play or will they have to play it safe? These decisions must be made almost instantly.

Then, look closely at the setter and the body cues this player may provide in determining where the set is headed. Typically, if the ball is far in front of the setter's head, chances are good he/she will set the ball to the outside. Conversely, if the ball is at the midline of the setter's body or if the setter's head or back is leaning backward, he/she will likely backset. In addition, some setters have a tendency to jump set when going to their middle attack.

After a decision is made as to where the set is going, the blocker must immediately pick up the attacker and read the body in order to determine where the shot is directed. Four rules when reading the attacker should be followed:

○ If the ball is inside the attacker's shoulder, chances are he/she will hit cross-court.

○ If the ball passes the midline of the attacker's body, chances are he/she will hit the seam or line.

○ If the set is tight, the blockers need to release earlier.

○ If the ball is set off the net, chances are it will be a high percentage attack (e.g., cross-court shot). In this situation, the blockers must delay to allow for the ball to travel from the point of contact to the net.

Finally, it is necessary to know the opponent's hitting tendencies. Do they hit straight ahead? Do they have a strong rotation of shoulders? What are their favorite shots? Do they pull the ball down when attacking?

Coaches should be responsible for this area, scouting the opponent prior to the competition. If pre-match scouting cannot be accomplished, the coach should watch the opponent during warm-up drills and in the first game of the match. But your players can also pick up these tendencies by watching the opponent.

DOUBLE BLOCK

Establishing a solid double block is critical to any team's blocking scheme. But this is not always easy since too many times the outside blocker wants to do his/her own thing. That is why it is imperative for the middle and outside blockers to work together.

• Outside blockers need to set the block while the middle blockers need to close and square their shoulders to the net.

• Outside blockers need to press hands into the middle blockers' to help seal the seam and redirect the ball into the court.

• The block must be timed together in order to form a solid, strong two-person block. If one player is going up while the other is coming down, the purpose of the block has been defeated. In this situation, the hitter will be able to use the block successfully.

• Middle blockers who are parallel to the net need to drop their inside hand in order to stop the cut shot when hit.

• Outside blockers need to reach into the seam as opposed to the middle blocker reaching out to close the block.

• Blockers must communicate the opponent's strategy. If a hitter is crossing, blockers must communicate where and to whose zone the attacker is entering.

THE SHORT AND TALL OF IT

As I mentioned before, if a team is not a strong, physical blocking team, it needs to be satisfied with channeling the block to the defense. But within this scheme, a setter can feel like he/she is not much value to the block because it does not show in the statistics. Coaches need to stress the importance of the setter's role in the block, whether it be slowing the ball down or successfully executing a soft block. The philosophy "I am short, therefore I cannot block" cannot exist in the mind of any of your players. A coach needs to be sure that all players understand their role within the blocking system. This will eliminate any self-doubt.

Conversely, the exceptionally tall athlete is often thought to be a great blocker. This is not always the case. These players need to learn how to penetrate the net to seal off more of the court and to avoid getting used by opponent. The key is to keep the hands above and close to the net in order to block and direct the ball. Their height allows them to stay above the net for a longer period of time.

Cathy George is the head women's volleyball coach at Western Michigan University in Kalamazoo, Mich.

"I think that reading the play is something that coaches have gotten away from a little bit; therefore, making blocking decisions based on the read is difficult.

The No. 1 responsibility of the blocker is to watch the pass off the passer's arms. Instead of just worrying about their responsibility in their zone, teach them to see each contact of the ball on the other side of the net beginning with the pass off of the passer's arms. If it is a good pass, they are in their normal blocking mode. But if it is a bad pass, they already have a decision made for them. For instance, a bad pass means the middle blocker releases outside. Every play is going to be dictated by how the pass goes."

(Greg Giovanazzi. Blocking at the collegiate level. *Coaching Volleyball*, April/May 1993, 10-13.)

Section VI: Serve Receive

Effective Serve Receive Techniques

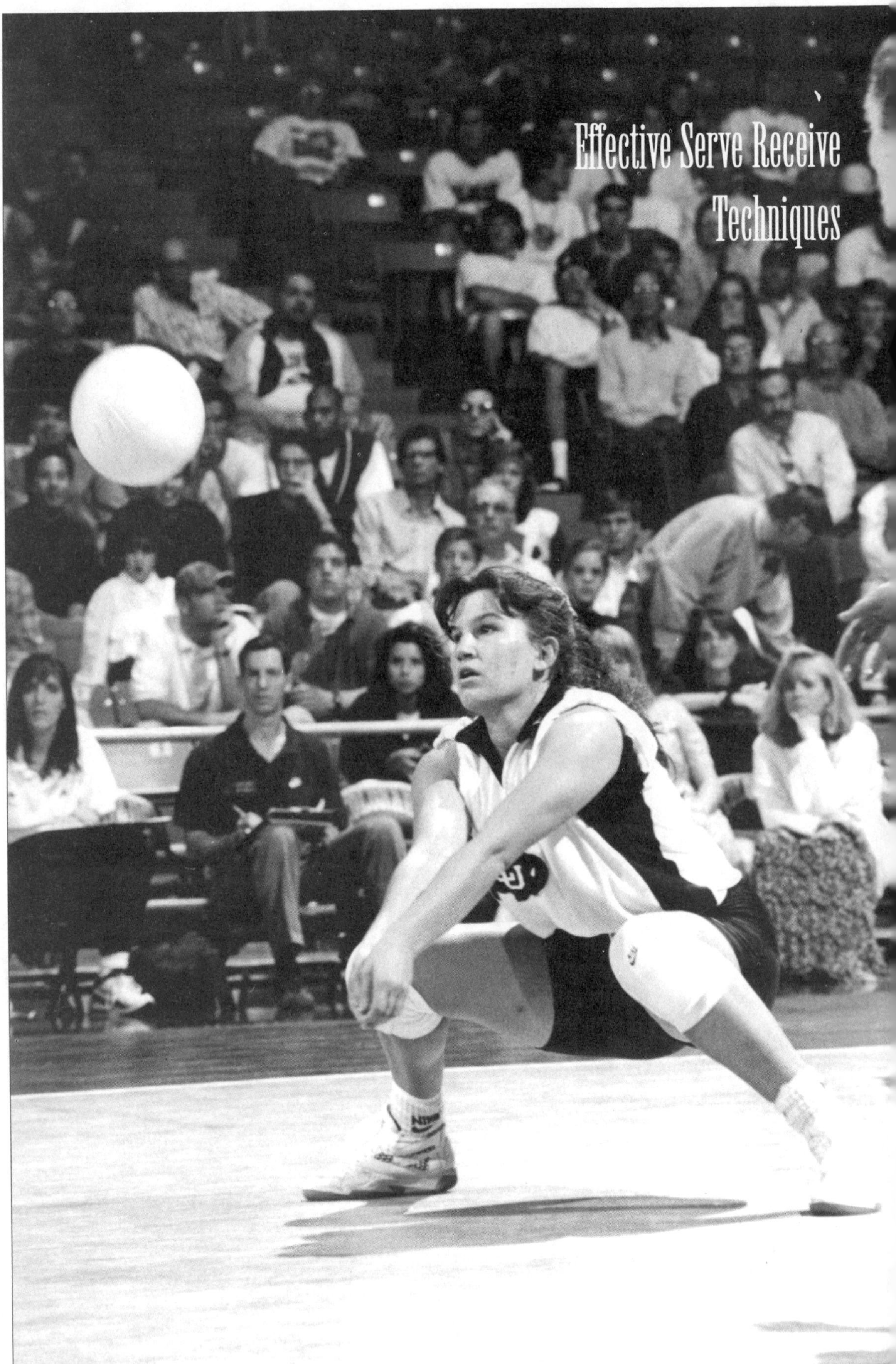

Effective Serve Receive Techniques

LOIS MUELLER

Serve receive is one of the most important phases of the volleyball match for two reasons. First, it provides an excellent opportunity for the receiving team to initiate an offensive system and attack. Since the receiving team knows the serve will be delivered, it can call plays, plan a specific offense or employ other tactics for successfully attacking the opponent. Secondly and conversely, serve receive is important because an error will result in a point for the opposing team. Because of these two factors, receiving serve is a major factor affecting match momentum.

According to Mueller, the receiving team knows many things about the serve which allow for control, prediction and intelligent decision making.

When receiving serve it is frequently thought that the server has all of the advantages—that the receiving team is at a clear disadvantage. While that may be true to a certain extent, it may not be as true as is initially suspected. When analyzed closely, the receiving team knows many things about the serve which allow for control, prediction and intelligent decision making. Thus the server does not "hold all the cards."

There are six "knowns" that the receiving team can count on and/or control when the ball is served to them. Each will be discussed in forthcoming paragraphs.

These knowns are:

1) when the ball will be served - **serve occurrence;**
2) what skill will be used to receive serve - **receiving skill**;
3) where the ball will be served from - **serve location**;
4) where they hope to deliver the ball to - **passing target**;
5) how the ball will be served - **types of serves**; and
6) who will receive the serve - **reception formation**.

SERVE OCCURRENCE

The receiving team always knows when the ball will be served. It cannot occur during a rally or as a surprise. The serve always takes place following a dead ball and after the official's whistle. Therefore, a routine can be developed to assist the receivers in being focused and ready. An example of a pre-reception routine is as follows: The official whistles for the serve and the receivers focus on the server; the server then tosses the ball and the receivers get down into their ready position:

whistle—> focus, toss—> down.

The receivers are then in the proper ready position, concentrating on the serve, ready to identify the type of serve and execute accordingly.

Not only does the pre-reception routine ensure that the receivers are ready, it also ensures that they do not tire too quickly by being ready too soon. Nearly twice as much time is spent with the ball dead as is spent with it in play during a typical volleyball match. If the receivers can be in the proper place on the court but relaxed until the official's whistle sounds, they will tire less quickly and focus more intently when it really matters.

Nearly twice as much time is spent with the ball dead as is spent with it in play during a typical volleyball match. If the receivers can be in the proper place on the court but relaxed until the official's whistle sounds, they will tire less quickly and focus more intently when it really matters.

RECEIVING SKILL

In almost every case, the serve will be handled with an underhand pass. Because of this it is not necessary to practice receiving serve using numerous skills; only underhand passing of the serve need be rehearsed. This greatly limits the variables involved. Underhand passing should be done with minimal arm movement prior to the actual passing of the ball. Habits such as bending the elbows, thereby bringing the hands up to the chest area then straightening the arms and passing, are unnecessary and may consume too much time prior to passing a rapidly moving serve.

A second important factor when underhand passing serve is to stand with the feet in a stride position and the right foot forward. Although this may run counter to the school of thought which states that the outside foot should always be forward, it is recommended because it allows for a shift of weight from the back left foot to the forward right foot. Every receiver, regardless of position on the court, must pass the ball to the right and therefore should be utilizing a weight shift from left to right. If the receiver has the left foot forward, the weight cannot be shifted to the right and toward the target.

SERVER LOCATION AND PASSING TARGET

The fact that every receiver must pass the ball to the right is based on knowing where the serve is coming from and to what target the ball should be passed. The rules require the server to deliver the ball from the right 1/3 of the court and behind the baseline. Receivers should always square their shoulders to the server, not to the baseline of the court. They will then pass the ball to the setter or target area, which is usually beside the net in the center of the court or just to the right of center. When the receiver's shoulders are squared to the server and the target area is at the net near the court or just to the right of center, the ball is always passed to the right (see Figures 1 and 2).

Choosing a target area which is immediately beside the net is another factor which should be given consideration. This target area may be best, especially for passing to a setter who will deliver quick sets and run numerous attack patterns. However, it does not allow any margin of error for passes which are long. Those passes will either go into the net or over the net, eliminating any attack possibilities. If the target area is moved toward the attack line, a margin of error for long passes is created. The setter can now move in all directions to get to passes which are not perfect, where previously the setter could only move in three directions. Though this target area is not as ideal and makes a quick attack more difficult, it should be considered when coaching teams that have difficulty passing serve and/or teams that run a basic offensive system.

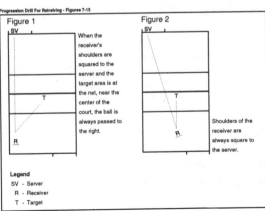

Progression Drill For Retreiving - Figures 7-15

Figure 1

SV

When the receiver's shoulders are squared to the server and the target area is at the net, near the center of the court, the ball is always passed to the right.

T

R

Figure 2

SV

T

R

Shoulders of the receiver are always square to the server.

Legend
SV - Server
R - Receiver
T - Target

TYPES OF SERVES

Most serves are of two types: floater or topspin. The proportion of floater to topspin serves varies with the area of the country, the level of play and the individual team. Careful observation and charting of the opponent may reveal that a high percentage of the serves to be received will be floaters or perhaps certain opposing teams will use all topspin serves. This information allows for prediction of what type of serve will have to be received. In addition, players can be taught to identify the type of serve while it is being executed and then respond accordingly. Spin or no spin is often sufficient information to distinguish floaters from topspin serves. Volleyballs of two or more colors make the recognition of spin quicker and easier when teaching players to identify the type of serve.

"Step and reach" are cue words players can use to receive a topspin serve effectively.

If the serve is delivered with topspin, the receiver should move into position and then step forward and reach with the arms. This additional movement toward the ball is made to adjust for the rapid and unexpected descent of a topspin serve. "Step and reach" are cue words which can be used by players.

When receiving a floater serve, the passer should move into position and then extend the arms over the left leg rather than in the center of the stance. This position allows the passer to raise the arms if the ball suddenly rises and a successful pass can still be executed. If the passer is attempting to contact the ball on arms extended in the center of the stance, no upward adjustment is possible. "Side" is a cue word which can be used when receiving floating serves.

RECEPTION FORMATION

Since the serve occurs after a dead ball and can be anticipated, the receiving team can use a formation which will be most successful for those players. Creative arranging can make it possible for the strongest receivers to handle the majority of the serves. Another factor when choosing a reception formation is that it may not be necessary to cover the entire court. Few servers can effectively and consistently serve to the right side of the opposing court or to the deep right back corner. Playing the odds and leaving these areas open, thereby making the area which must be covered smaller, is strongly recommended. These open areas often tempt servers to attempt very difficult serves and commit errors.

When designing these formations, the coach should use caution if placing very aggressive players beside each other. It may prove more beneficial to position a less-aggressive -- yet skilled -- passer next to a very aggressive and talented passer.

CONCLUSION

Many factors can be determined or predicted when receiving serve. Six of these factors or "knowns" were discussed in the preceding paragraphs. Recognizing these factors greatly minimizes the variables which must be dealt with and enhances the opportunities to receive serve successfully.

Lois Mueller is a volleyball coach from Mequon, Wis.

The Mobile, Two-Layered
Serve Reception System

The Mobile, Two-Layered Serve Reception System

IRADGE AHRABI-FARD AND
SHARON HUDDLESTON

A carefully calculated plan for service reception can strengthen the offensive performance of any volleyball team. Even though a good pass is an essential part of the offense, it is the service reception system that turns passing into the precursor of a forceful offense. An effective service reception system must combine the passing strengths and weaknesses of the players and the court positions of the setter(s) and attackers in order to maximize the collective passing potential of a team.

An effective service reception system combines passing strengths and setter/attacker court positions to maximize the collective passing potential of a team.

Most players excel in the skill of serving earlier than they acquire the skill of passing the service accurately to a target. Developing good passing technique, however, does not automatically result in an effective serve reception. It takes years to incorporate service reception into the offense by learning to pass the serve consistently and accurately. Designing and developing a successful service reception system that parallels the passing skill of players and other specifics of the team is an arduous process for a coach, but well worth the time required. As many coaches have found, top NCAA Division I teams that do not have effective service reception systems can be quickly taken out of the game by lesser skilled service-oriented teams.

There are several principles that underlie any service reception system. Considerable thought and planning time, for instance, should be allocated in order to:

✱Determine the portion of the court that needs to be covered for the reception of each serve.

✱Design a logical formation to cover the intended area of the court with either one or two layers of passers.

✱Identify the primary passers in each rotation.

✱Specify each passer's coverage area and responsibility.

✱Manipulate the overlap rules in order to position the passers, the setter and designated attackers in their most advantageous areas.

✱Establish passing priorities for each rotation.

✱Establish the linear (mid-line of the body) or non-linear (side of the body) passing preference for each player (e.g., players in the left 2/3 of the court should use either a linear pass or a left-to-right non-linear pass. A right-to-right non-linear pass is prone to error.)

> Designing and developing a successful service reception system that parallels the passing skill of players and other specifics of the team is an arduous process for a coach, but well worth the time required.

✱Teach the passers the necessary court behavior in relation to their position prior to receiving the serve and during service reception (e.g., ready posture, reading the serve, movement, communication and balance.)

✱Determine positions and responsibilities for the non-passers in the service reception formation.

✱Design an alternative plan to be used if the service reception system fails (e.g., three service aces or free balls in succession would indicate the reception system has failed and may require an alternative system.)

THE TWO-LAYER SERVICE RECEPTION SYSTEM

Recently, two- and three-passer service reception systems have become a popular concept. A one-layer system of two or three passers, however, must cover the depth, as well as the width of the court and, therefore, has a built-in weakness. An effective strategy against a one-layer service reception system is to concentrate on one player's position on the court, forcing the player to cover the entire distance from the net to the end line. This strategy is more suitable for the women's game, however, as short serves are more difficult to execute in the men's game due to the height of the net. In the women's game, then, the use of this service strategy can result in service reception failure of a one-layer system.

The more concentrated two-layer system contains two layers or rows of passers that are capable of adjusting their court positions according to their perceptions of the server's intentions. As a matter of fact, the two-layer system is especially effective when a server telegraphs the intended target. The two-layer system also offers a more balanced court coverage, as well as allowing for the best passing options. This system of service reception is very flexible and could be used either as a secondary option or as the primary service reception system of a team.

There are a number of ways to organize a two-layer service reception system. For example, a coach might choose to use five passers, four passers or three passers in the system. In this article, however, the intent is to introduce variations of a mobile, four-passer system which includes:

1. The U formation—the basic starting formation for service reception in which the back layer stays inside the front layer (see Figure 1);

2. The N formation—in which the two layers shift their positions so that the front layer is closer to the right side of the court while the back layer is closer to the left side (see Figure 2);

3. The reverse N formation— in which the two layers shift their positions so that the front layer is closer to the left while the back player is

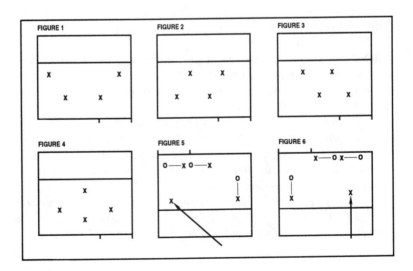

closer to the right side of the court (see Figure 3);

4. The pie formation—in which one passer covers short while three passers cover deep (see Figure 4).

A two-layer system of four passers balances the court coverage. The advantage of the mobile system is that the passers are able to adjust their positions to afford very effective coverage to either the right or left side of the court and from the net to the baseline. The initial formation for service reception is the two-layered formation followed by player movement (position adjustment) that is based on the body position of the server. As the server selects a target, she/he usually shows the intended direction of the serve by stance adjustment and body posture (shoulders). Effective servers usually do not attempt to conceal their service intentions. Any effort to change service posture or technique in order to disguise intentions would adversely affect the accuracy and consistency of an effective serve. The two deep receivers in the U formation should interpret the server's intention and communicate the information to their teammates. Regardless of which formation is called for after the U, the movement of the players is prearranged. Both deep receivers should take a quick slide step toward the direction of the serve to form a passing triangle with the front-row passer who is closest to the intended target. In this passing triangle, the two back players would pass the deep serves while the front layer passer would pass the short serves. The other front layer passer would fall back to balance and cover the third of the court vacated by the two deep passers. This positioning is necessary in order to cover the possibility of the unexpected (either accidental or change of intent) deep serve. If players are not able to read the intention of the server, they should hold their U positions and stay focused in order to be able to react appropriately during the toss. For predictable servers, the coach or players could designate an "N" or a reverse "N" starting formation and then adjust if the server indicates a different target.

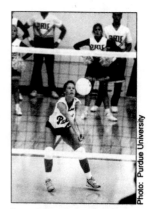

Passers learn to focus on the behavior of the server in this system.

In Figures 5 and 6, the player's starting position is shown by "X", their movement is shown by a line and their adjusted position is shown by "0".

The major advantages of the mobile, two-layered service reception system are:

1. Passers learn to focus on the behavior of the server.

2. Passers will learn to communicate for the best possible collective effort.

3. By moving toward the target area, it is communicated to the server that the target area has been recognized. This may disturb the server's focus.

4. There will be less area to cover against a fast serve.

5. There will be less movement getting to the serve, hence more attention is paid to the quality of the pass.

6. The depth of the serve is covered by two layers.

7. In each rotation, one weak passer may be hidden.

8. The back row setter can often be brought to the net, nearer to the setting area.

9. The best passers may be given priorities within this system.

10. This system of serve reception may be used as an option in conjunction with other systems.

The major disadvantage of the two-layer system is the difficulty of coordinating the front receivers with the back receivers. If the players are not properly instructed, the front-row passers could interfere with the back-row passers. Considerable practice time is required to overcome this potential problem.

Because position serving is effective even against many Division I college teams, it is the responsibility of a coach to design a sound service reception system that has the potential of neutralizing the threat of an accurate server. The four-passer mobile service reception system is a definite option that can give a team the edge against an effective position server who is capable of serving short as well as deep.

Iradge Ahrabi-Fard is the head women's volleyball coach at the University of Northern Iowa in Cedar Falls, Iowa. Sharon Huddleston is an associate professor and sport psychologist at the University of Northern Iowa.

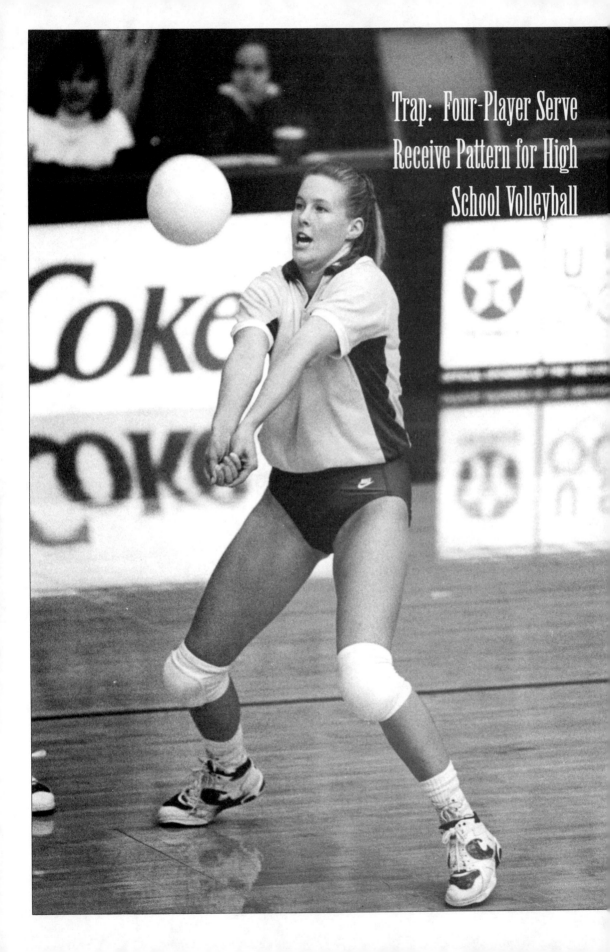

Trap: Four-Player Serve
Receive Pattern for High
School Volleyball

Trap: Four-Player Serve Receive Pattern for High School Volleyball

M. Eileen Mathews

The trap is an efficient serve-receive formation using a parallelogram configuration of four primary receivers that minimizes seams, limits decision-making, protects the court's major areas and provides shift options—and, with all this, improves serve-receive performance.

With high school volleyball players getting better at varying the type and controlling the direction of their serves, it has become progressively harder to defense the serve with the serve-receive, minimize errors and convert to offense.

Four primary receivers are used in the trap, which improves serve receive performance.

SETTING THE TRAP

Using four primary receivers in two offsetting lines of two players each, you can set the trap with a front-line shift to the right (see Figure 1) to protect center court and cross court better or a front-line shift to the left to protect against the line serve better (see Figure 2). The two remaining players are released from reception duties. Decide which players to exclude from the reception formation according to the strengths and weaknesses of the team, offensive strategies and service efficiency of the opposition.

With a 5-1 offense, the primary objective is to place the setter nearest the set target area, so she/he should not receive serve. When starting from the back row, the setter comes to the net to a position that lets her/him more efficiently initiate the offense. She/he is free to assume any advantageous position within the confines of the overlap rules.

Because the player directly in front of the setter must also advance to the net, the setter should be positioned near the attack line for two reasons: One, the player in front must have room to begin an approach. Two, the setter's assumed position around the attack line deceives the server, who sees the setter as part of the serve receive. In actuality, the setter should be ready (and is in position) to play the short serve.

With the setter in a front-row position, transition to offense is simpli-

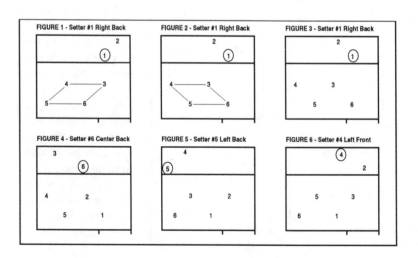

fied. The setter takes an inside path between the net and the remaining front-row players to the target area. One of the remaining two players can be designated as the primary attacker while the other accepts passing responsibilities as a member of the trap.

The trap's second objective is to provide a quick attack, dictating that a hitter be released from reception duties. When the setter initiates transition from the back row, the player directly in front becomes the attacker. Similarly, a weak passer can be released from serve-receive duties.

You must determine the priority between operating a quick attack or strengthening serve-receive by releasing a player from passing duties, for the two are interrelated. Because only one player can be pulled from the serve-receive along with the setter, the remaining players must fulfill passing responsibilities.

The final objective of the trap -- and its major advantage -- is to make it easy for players to shift to protect the court better, assist a player who is having trouble passing, facilitate the offense or simply deceive the server. Figures 3 through 11 define the serve-receive (and some offensive options) for all players in each of the six serve-receive rotations while executing a 5-1 offense.

Figure 3 depicts the relative positions of players when the setter plays from the right back. To place her/him near the target area, player 2 (preferably a middle or weakside hitter) must advance toward the net to comply with overlap rules.

There is some flexibility for hitter 2 horizontally as long as she/he remains inside or to the right of player 3 (again, in compliance with overlap rules). The four other players may be deployed in a left shift as shown. They may also be deployed in a right shift, but this tends to place player 2 very near the sideline and would probably preclude her/him from becoming a strongside hitter.

Figure 4 shows player positions when the setter initiates play from the center of the back row. Player 3 must be closer to the net than the setter; in this position she/he can run a middle or an outside attack.

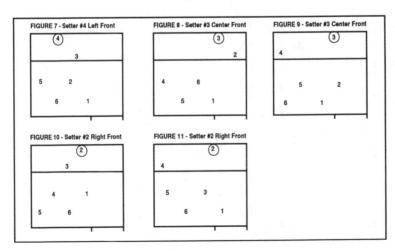

Figure 5 illustrates the setter playing from the left back. This is the most difficult starting position. Player 4 is the obvious hitter and is able to assume an easy outside approach. However, a middle attack can also be initiated from this posture.

In Figures 6 and 7 the setter is finally able to operate from a service rotation position in the front row as she/he starts from the left front. This rotation provides two hitter options and lets you use either the left or right serve-receive shift.

Figure 6 designates the option with player 2 as a hitter. A weakside or left-handed hitter is ideal in this situation. The middle attack can be executed as well. In Figure 7, player 3 should be a strong middle attacker or an outside hitter. The right-shift serve-receive with the remaining four players facilitates the 5-1 offense here.

Figures 8 and 9 detail options for offense, as well as for serve-receive. With the setter operating from center front, player 2 or 4 can be chosen as a hitter. If player 2 is chosen, a left-shift receive follows. If player 4 is the primary hitter, an outside attack is best facilitated, along with a right-shift receive. The final rotation with the setter in the right front (see Figure 10) again provides two options. Player 3 or 4 can be used for the attack. With player 3 either the outside attack or middle attack is available. If player 4 is the primary attacker (see Figure 11), she/he may also choose to attack from the middle or from the weak side.

ADVANTAGES OF THE TRAP

The trap was designed to overcome or improve upon the vulnerable aspects of traditional serve-receive patterns and to provide players with a means to make viable adjustments that would affect the server and improve performance. The trap has many advantages over other serve-receive formations:

▲Areas of responsibility are specifically defined (due to the staggered positioning of players).

▲ Overlapping of those responsibilities is minimal.

▲ Communication with other receivers is not as critical because no player is beside or directly behind another.

▲ If a team serves short, the setter or hitter can easily back off the net and protect the attack line area.

▲ A simple shift lets the forward or backward player protect against the line serve.

▲ The cross-court service area, which receives the most serves at the high school level, is protected by two players, as is the midcourt area.

▲ Some seams are eliminated by reducing the number of passers from five to four.

▲ Position shifts are easily accomplished without much attention to overlap.

The trap is a more complete receiving formation, with unique advantages and greater flexibility than the standard serve-receive patterns (the M, the W, the Triangle, the Dish, the Box). The trap alignment was effective with both our varsity's 5-1 offense and the junior varsity's 6-2 offense. Its advantages provide a viable, effective serve-receive at the high school level.

M. Eileen Mathews is a coach with the East Valley School District in Yakima, Wash., and is a USA Volleyball CAP certified coach.

Serve Receive Specialization

Serve Receive Specialization

SEAN MADDEN

Because of some serious defensive flaws and middle attacking errors, your team has just lost an important match. Your next match, two days away, is against a tough serving team—and your squad is notorious for self-destructing on serve receive. What can you do in just two hours' practice time to avert this ugly scene?

You cannot work miracles, but you can show your players how to improve their serve receive skills in a minimum of time, which, in turn, will let them work on other skills, as well.

How? By using fewer passers in your serve receive. Make your best passers "designated ballhogs." The resulting greater efficiency is a matter of simple mathematics: The same amount of drill time divided among fewer passers playing fewer positions equals more practice per passer per position. I will spell this out in detail after we look at the history of specialization in volleyball and its relationship to training efficiency.

Madden believes using fewer passers in your serve receive will result in greater efficiency.

THE HISTORY OF SPECIALIZATION

Specialization began in volleyball with the advent of designated setters (rather than the second-ball player becoming the "setter," as still is common in Sunday picnic volleyball). Coaches designated setters because they recognized that some players could set better than others and that it was much more efficient to train a couple of players—not the whole team—to set.

Offensive specialization was the next move. Innovative coaches saw major differences in attacking from the left side versus the middle and the right. So to reduce the demand on any one player and to get more out of training time, coaches began having players always switch front-row positions to attack from the same position along the net.

Defensive specialization followed shortly after. It only made sense to switch players in the backcourt so that they could dig from one position and, again, reap the greatest benefits from training time.

These developments of specialization resulted in greater training efficiency: Each player trained in fewer positions and the training time for each position was divided among fewer players.

SERVE RECEIVE SPECIALIZATION

The traditional "W" serve receive has been questioned in recent years at all levels of the game. Many coaches have seen the wisdom of removing the middle attacker from the receive formation to allow a better approach for the quick attack—but usually this same player is part of the reception pattern when she's in the back row, so she still needs her share of limited serve receive training time. Only in the 1980s teams began to limit the number of players who would pass a served ball in competition. Most notably, serve receive specialization played a key in the rise of our men's national team to the No. 1 world position. In the 1980s, Karch Kiraly, Aldis Berzins and Bob Ctvrtlik became internationally renowned for their impeccable two-man reception. If you watch any women's NCAA Division I teams you see a variety of two-, three- and four-person recep-

Fewer receivers simplify communication and reduce confusion.

tion patterns, but seldom five or anything close to a "W."

At the highest levels of play serve receive specialization is now the rule, not the exception. For the same reasons that it has become common at the top, it should become the standard of play at all levels.

DESIGNATION OF SERVE RECEIVE SPECIALISTS

Serve receive specialization should be used at all levels for several reasons. First, serve receive is as important a skill as exists in volleyball. A team that cannot pass serve will not sideout and a team that cannot sideout will lose. Given its importance, every possible step should be taken to ensure the most effective serve reception.

Second, as with any skill, certain players perform better than others. Some teams are blessed with several good passers while others struggle to find one, but there are distinctions in every group.

Third, five players are not needed to cover the court on serve receive—in a game of doubles, two players can cover the whole court most of the time! Three players in a 9 x 9 meter area is plenty. Four is very safe. Five is often a crowd.

Which leads us to the fourth reason: Fewer receivers simplify communication and reduce confusion. Most aces against a five-person receive are not caused by an inability to reach the ball but by hesitation among the passers ("I have it—you take it"). Fewer players mean less traffic. Besides, nonpassers can learn to be excellent air traffic controllers, calling lines and the name of the most appropriate passer as the serve comes over.

Fifth, passing, like any skill, improves with successful repetitions. The more served balls that a player passes effectively from a position on the court, the more skilled she/he will become in passing future balls from that position. For a player to reach and maintain her/his athletic potential, specific repetitions are crucial.

A team that cannot pass serve will not sideout and a team that cannot sideout will lose. Given its importance, every possible step should be taken to ensure the most effective serve reception.

REDUCED NUMBERS OF RECEIVERS

If you can accept these reasons, you should have no problem understanding the merits of using fewer players in serve receive. Let me, as an example, describe the advantages of a three-person receive, which seems ideal for the women's game.

For a three-person receive, the coach selects three of six starters to pass every ball. In a 5-1 offense the usual three are the outside attackers, leaving the middles to focus on running the quick attack. The coach will need to train substitutes, but usually they are limited to the backup outside attackers and the defensive specialists. For the sake of explaining the mathematical advantages, I discuss only the training of starters here, but the advantages are identical in training substitutes.

If your typical practice includes serving 90 balls to your starting serve receivers, each receives 18 contacts in the traditional five-person pattern. Using a three-person receive, each player averages 30 contacts—a 67% increase.

In the five-person receive, the 18 contacts per player are divided among five passing positions to average 3.6 contacts per player per position. In the three-person, if each player trains in all three positions, there are 10 contacts per player per position—nearly three times more. Because it is simple to deploy three passers so that each plays only two positions in the pattern, the contacts per player per position can be increased to 15.

To this number superiority you can add the intangibles of playing alongside and becoming familiar with just two players rather than four. Because the 90 serves will take no more time than usual, serve receive training has been increased without adding practice time. In fact, the number of serves could be reduced with still more specific repetitions per passer and more time to focus on other areas of training. Either way, team serve receive will improve.

If you choose a four-person receive, the mathematical advantages diminish but still exist. If you go with a two-person, the advantages improve but you must consider whether two passers can effectively cover the whole court.

ANSWERING THE OBJECTIONS

Despite the math, some coaches disagree with reduced numbers on serve receive. Their objections are worthy of note and of response.

Some high school and club coaches argue that players who are not allowed to serve receive will not be "complete" players and may be less recruitable. The middle player in this three-person line passes the ball as other primary passers open up the passing lane.

To the first part of this argument I respond that the "all-around" player is a thing of the past. If complete players are the goal, why have designations like "middle," "outside" and "setter"? Players trained to do everything often become all-around average players. Eliminating extensive serve-receive training from a player's practice schedule frees her to focus on and hone other important skills. For example, while three players are serve-receiving, the middles can be working with the setter to perfect the quick attack. In this way the whole team becomes stronger.

As for recruitability, a scholarship is more likely to be offered to a great attacker who does not pass than to an average attacker forced to regularly display her mediocre passing abilities. And a scholarship will more likely be rewarded to a successful passing specialist than to one who is just part of the reception crowd (given equal abilities in other areas).

A second major objection is very legitimate: A player will never improve in a skill that she never practices. But I would add that she must practice that skill in an optimal fashion in an optimal environment.

Serve receive is not the best way to develop passing skills except in advanced stages. The speed and movement of the ball tend to encourage bad habits among weak passers and they ingrain in many a sense of frustration and failure. And five bodies in a small area often results in timidity among the weaker passers. Until a player is a smooth, comfortable,

According to Bob Maxwell in his article titled "Siding Out With a Two- or Three-Person Receive" (*Coaching Volleyball*, August/Spetember 1990), "Specialization is an outstanding idea because it can capitalize on each player's strengths while hiding weaknesses. But the most overlooked area regarding specialization is serve reception.

Coaches look at players' abilities at the net (spiking and blocking) and decide where they should play. We design defenses to let our best defensive players dig the most balls and offenses to give our best hitters the most opportunities to attack with their best shots. But when it comes to serve reception (our primary means of preventing our opponents from scoring), we often just tell our players to pass to the target. We practice team serve receive for hours, but we defeat all of this practice because we still leave the targets (poor receivers) out on the court for our opponents to serve to."

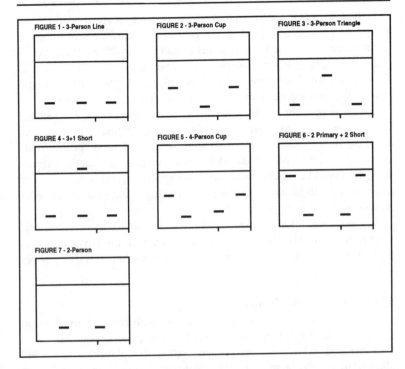

and confident passer, she will make greater gains in ball-handling drills than in actual serve receive. Ball-handling drills (two players passing various distances and heights and with varying movement) is repetition-intensive and should be included in every practice. In 10 minutes of ball-handling, a developing passer will get many more repetitions and can develop more ingrained success than in an hour of five-person serve receive.

A player wanting to become a stronger passer can then make great strides in the off-season by playing doubles or having serve and serve receive competitions with a friend. This allows her to develop passing skills without the pressure of letting five teammates down in important competitlon.

SERVE RECEPTION PATTERNS

Once convinced that fewer serve receivers is the future for a team, a coach has many options. Three-person patterns can take the form of a cup, a straight line or a triangle. The most typical four-person reception formations are the cup and the box. A two-person pattern leaves few options because the court must simply be divided in half.

A coach will want to consider each formation's coverage advantages. Factors include what directions players must move to reach a ball; how areas of responsibility are designated; how difficult communication is among the passers; and whether the placement of the front-row attackers who are passers makes it difficult for them to obtain a strong approach.

Coaches must also consider the court placement of nonreceivers. The primary concern is for the front-row players to get optimum approaches without creating traffic problems for the serve receivers. Another concern is to have nonpassers close to the lines so that they can call them for the serve receivers.

After experimenting on paper for awhile, you might be surprised at the leeway you have in moving players around without violating overlap rules. In time you will discover the pattern best suited to your personnel and offensive system.

Though you, like the rest of us, will continue to struggle with how to best spend your precious practice time, you should find that training fewer passers makes you more efficient and brings you closer to the team success that you desire.

Sean Madden is the head women's volleyball coach at Gonzaga University in Spokane, Wash., and is a USA Volleyball CAP certified coach.

Section VII: Defense

A solid floor defense may not bring the crowd to its feet as often as a crushing spike or block, but it can be just as important in earning a victory. Outstanding floor defense can produce points and change or solidify momentum—vital ingredients in a winning formula. A team should pick up three to five points per game directly from its floor defense and a great dig or save, especially in a tight situation, can inspire your team and deflate your opponent. Conversely, missing an easy defensive play could start your team on a tailspin that is hard to stop.

When installing a floor defense, a coach should be concerned with five factors: attitude, techniques, tactics, communication and pursuit-and-relay responsibilities.

According to Neville, as long as the ball is in the air it is assumed playable.

ATTITUDE

Defense is an attitude. Players must make a total commitment to the fact that every ball is playable and give a sincere, maximum effort to get to every ball. No value judgments on whether a ball is unplayable are tolerated. As long as the ball is in the air it is assumed playable and players must react accordingly. Stress pursuit -- relentless pursuit.

Players respect teammates who always give maximum effort. Pursuing defense is the single most demonstrable behavior of intensity. You can garner many game and match points through continual defensive prowess.

TECHNIQUES

Volleyball is played in three different body posture ranges. The high range includes spiking, blocking and jump setting. In the middle range are serve receiving, overhead passing and serving. The low range includes digging, collapse setting and desperation saves. Successful floor defense demands ball control, body control, mobility and balance in the low range.

Defense is an attitude. Players must make a total commitment to the fact that every ball is playable and give a sincere, maximum effort to get to every ball.

To achieve comfortable low-range posture, players must assume correct posture each time a defensive stance is required. Low position is achieved by bending at the knees. Knees are inside and in front of the big toes. The weight is forward, the heels and head are up and the back is straight. This posture allows balance, mobility and maximum arm range relative to rebound angle. Arms should be relaxed with the hands inside and slightly in front of the knees with the palms up. The player in the angles should have toes pointed directly across the court. Players should be relaxed, not tense or locked into the posture. The players' focus, however, is intense.

Players must also be aware of floor position. At the time of spiker contact they should be in position in an area most likely to be attacked. Furthermore, the defense should be in a position so that the ball cannot hit the court behind the digger and he or she can play the ball in front toward help. Also, the defensive player must see the ball being hit; thus,

Photo: Bates College

A coach should adjust defensive personnel based on an opponent's arsenal.

he or she must be in an open corridor or seam unless assigned to play in the block shadow to cover tip or deep deflections.

TACTICS

The floor defense, in most systems, must build around the block and what the block is doing (see Figures 1-7). Also, players must recognize that the block has back-row responsibility. The diggers should not feel

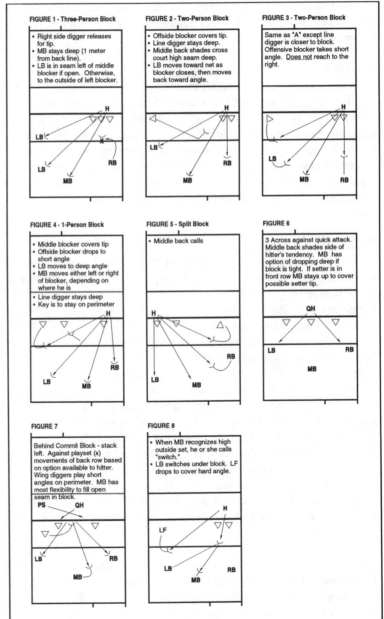

compelled to dig the whole court.

The basic tactical principles of floor defense are these:

• Put your best digger in the area most likely to be attacked.

• Players should always be in an on-help position, keeping teammates on the court side of them (players in the wing position should face cross-court).

• Be in correct digging posture at the moment of attack.

The principle of putting the best diggers in the areas most likely to be attacked requires switching diggers when possible. The obvious left-side attack is an example of a situation that allows you to switch. Your most mobile digger should play middle back and therefore you should try to have your two best diggers opposite each other. Because at any level of volleyball a right-handed attacker will hit cross-court 80% of the time, a switch is made as follows when the obvious left-side attack is recognized (see Figure 8): The middle back calls "switch." The left-back player releases to cover the tip under the block and the left-front player (the other best defensive player) drops back into the power angle. The result is that the best diggers are in the areas most likely to be attacked. All teams usually attack from their left, especially in tight situations. The switch defense is designed to load up on this attack.

As you look at each rotation you must determine your best diggers and where they perform best. In addition, you should adjust your defensive personnel based upon your opponent's arsenal and how they will deploy in any given situation.

A back-row player is given the responsibility of setting the defense. This player must consider the other players' ability to get into position. For example, it may not be possible to get the server switched to the left back position because that would limit the serve or cause him or her to be ineffective against the fast attack. Switching is also limited when the setter, because of transition responsibility, needs to play right back.

Switching decisions are made based on opponent tendencies within a rotation in certain situations:

• In tight situations after 12 points;

• After a hitter gets blocked one or more times;

•When the quick attack has been shut down or is going well;

•When the general flow of the game is "normal" (e.g., first 10 points, few pressure situations); and

• When a front-row sub enters the game.

Switches can be made by the coach during a time-out or by the responsible player prior to the serve. A simple switch (middle and left back or middle and right back) can be called by the responsible person on a bad pass situation when a high ball to the opponent's No. 4 hitter is the only logical option.

COMMUNICATION

There must be ongoing, clear, concise communication during all defensive situations, coupled with consistent adherence to the rules of defense. The same trigger word also must be used by all players for appropriate situations. For example, a player about to make contact should always call "mine" or "ball." If a second player is in close contact and there may be hesitation, the words, "yours," "okay," or "go" signal the player who called the ball that it is his or hers. The communication sequence is:

1) Direction (before each play defenders review their responsibilities based on the situation);

2) possession ("Mine!"); and

3) confirmation ("Yours!").

One of the most devastating palls that can be cast over a team's tempo results from losing a point or scoring opportunity because of a failure in communication. To reduce the chances of such failures, one designated player in the back row should be responsible for directing that row.

PURSUIT-AND-RELAY RESPONSIBILITIES

The block should be touching many attacked balls. Some will be terminal ricochets, but most, you hope, will be deflected so that back-row defensive pursuit is possible. The usual deflection that can be pursued goes deep out of the court. Most often the middle back defender, by virtue of position, will have first-contact pursuit responsibility. The wing digger closest to the trajectory follows, prepared to make the second contact. The rest of the team should automatically move toward the pursuit in preparation for the third contact.

If the ball is deflected off the block out of bounds, the wing digger nearest the ball pursues, followed by the middle back defender. Pursuit by every player is the absolute necessity.

RULES OF DEFENSE AND BALL HANDLING

✳The player farthest from and facing the target plays the ball.

✳ Players should always play the ball in front of themselves.

✳ Players should be stopped, weight forward, just prior to the attack.

✳ Players should play in the on-help position.

✳ All defenders must know second-contact responsibility.

✳ The off-side blocker who cannot establish a strong defensive position automatically covers the tip.

SUMMARY

Outstanding floor defense can often turn a volleyball match around. Careful attention to teaching floor defense fundamentals is essential to preparing a successful team.

Bill Neville is the head women's volleyball coach at the University of Washington in Seattle, Wash., and was the assistant coach for the U.S. men's national team that won the gold medal at the 1984 Olympic Games in Los Angeles, Calif. Neville is a USA Volleyball CAP certified coach.

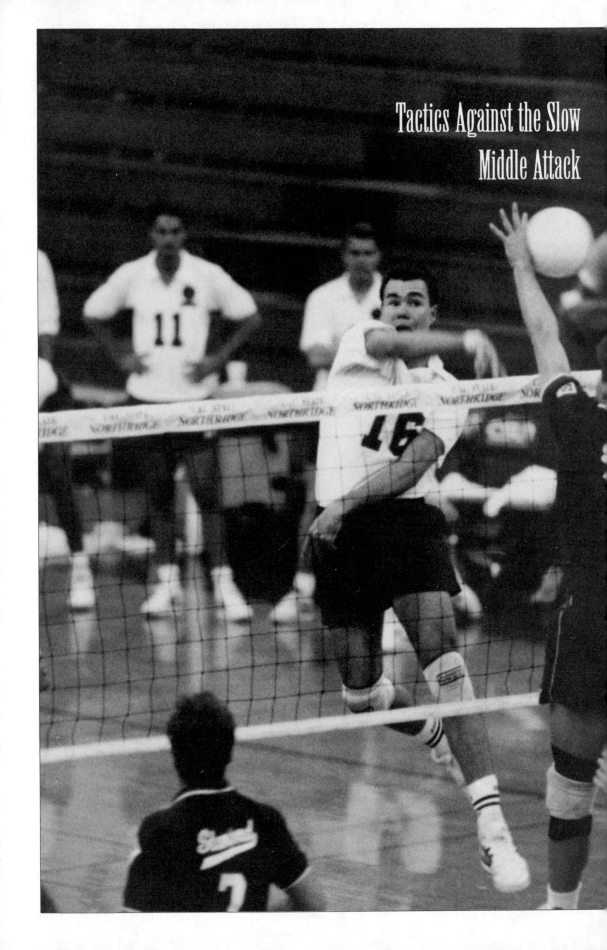

Tactics Against the Slow Middle Attack   Tim Davison

At many levels of play, the high middle set (2 set or 53) is still the primary middle attack set used. Even with teams using a "quicker" game, the middle is often used for a "quick-and-a-half" set which floats about 3 feet above the net waiting for the hitter to arrive and swing at it. Both of these sets are easily blocked. A double block is one choice. The article that follows deals with block positioning and responsibilities and transition from defense to offense.

Block positioning and the transition from defense to offense are key tactics against the slow middle attack.

BASIC BLOCKING RESPONSIBILITIES

Our blocking formation is known as a "bunch" formation (see Figure 1). Our left-front blocker is approximately eight feet in from the left antenna; our middle blocker is slightly to the left of center court — toward the opponent's primary setting area; and our right-front blocker is 8 to 10 feet in from the right sideline. Our right-front blocker is usually a converted middle blocker. We are looking for size and blocking experience plus the basic ability to secondary set the ball high out to the left side. If the right-side player is your setter, many more set options become available.

The left-front blocker is our main communicator calling out information to the other players on the court—front- or back-row setter, number of hitters, their numbers and pointing out their court positions—split hitters, strong right or left, stack, etc. If the opponent's setter is front-row, our left-front blocker has "dump responsibility" and will stay in front of the setter watching for clues.

Our middle blocker identifies the opponent's middle hitter and watches for cues on movement. The player is also cognizant of the pass and will begin to "cheat" outside on a bad pass—one that virtually eliminates a quick or middle attack. On a good pass, he/she concentrates on the middle attacker and any movement toward the middle attack area by opponent hitters.

The right-front blocker stays home until a decision is made on the options off the pass. If the pass is to the setting area, she/he takes one short slide step toward the middle, attempting to pick up the approach route of the middle attacker while waiting for the setter's decision. If the pass forces a high outside set, he/she finds the outside attacker and moves to the right to intercept the approach.

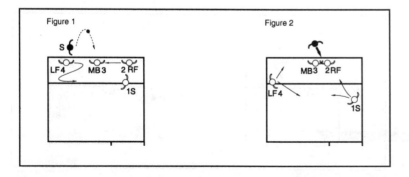

A variety of sets can be run from the formation Davison describes.

BLOCKING THE SLOW MIDDLE

We double block the slow middle attack right side in. Many coaches choose to block left side and middle, but for transition purposes, we choose to double block with our middle blocker and right side blocker even if the right side blocker is our setter. As was mentioned earlier, we are looking for a right side blocker (not our primary setter) who is big with blocking experience. We believe that a big double block in the middle will force the opponents hitter to examine other options than just swinging away all the time. Our middle blocker is the primary blocker with the right-front player as the assist blocker.

We can ask our double block to do several things, depending on the personnel involved or the type of hitter we are blocking. We sometimes form a "cup" block and try to roof the hitter—especially if the hitter has a variety of angles to which she/he hits (see Figure 2). We also area or "channel" block whereby we will take away one area and force the hitter to go to an area where our backcourt players will be stationed. Or, when our "short" setter is assist blocking, we may soft block and work the attack up into the air and transition off the pass.

Many coaches have asked if it is worth the gamble on the setter's hands to block her/him in the middle. I have yet to lose a setter's fingers blocking right side in because a right-handed middle hitter has a somewhat difficult time cutting the ball with power back across her/his body. I have, however, lost setters on the outside against hitters who turn the ball hard down the line. Depending on the size and aggressiveness of your primary setter, you can make the decision of "stuff" or "soft" blocking techniques.

TRANSITION WITH SETTER IN THE BACK ROW

We run a 5-1 offense with a quick attacker on every pass possible. If the attack is played by anyone other than our setter (positioned in the right back), we release our setter up the sideline (one or two steps) and in at the attack line to the setting area. Our right front assist blocker opens left and drop or slide steps straight back to the attack line (see Figure 3). Our middle (primary) blocker opens right, finds the ball and crosses over to somewhere near the attack line, ready to explode to the setter for a quick attack on the good pass. Do not allow your middle attacker to slide

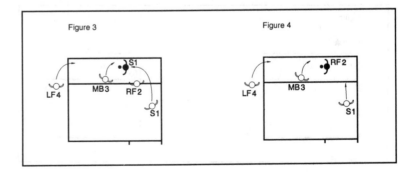

along the net to the left. She/he must get off the net to give the setter an angle to see her/him. Our left-side power hitter has dropped off the net to a position near, but not on, the left side line and approximately 10-12 feet off the net. The hitter turns and faces the court and digger and, when satisfied the "shank" responsibilities are over, back slide steps to the outside hitting position.

Reviewing Figure 3, you will see that we can run a variety of sets from this formation. The right front player can run a back quick, a slide quick, a back two set or an X2 set. The middle attacker can run a regular quick, the short shoot, the flare (tight or wide), a high middle two set or a high back two off the right front's quick (reverse "X"). The outside hitter is your safety set or you can give her/him whatever set he/she is capable of hitting.

If the setter (RB) handles the first ball, he/she simply passes the ball to the right side blocker (naturally opening to the left) and he/she (the RF) can set high outside or high into the middle.

TRANSITION WITH SETTER IN THE FRONT ROW

The transition here is quite simple (see Figure 4). You simply eliminate the right front. The setter opens left and slide steps to the setting area which is usually 3 feet away. The middle and outside attackers follow the same footwork patterns as before. The right-back player now becomes a back-row attacker.

Note that in a left-side in blocking scheme your outlet hitter (the left-front player) is much further away from the approach area. Also note that the setter is off the net and more susceptible to handling the first ball on a tip. Where is your secondary setter? Deep in the court when the setter is front row. When the setter is back row and one blocks left side in, the right-front player drops off the net, forcing the setter (RB) deeper back and further still from the setting area.

SUMMARY

As the game of volleyball gets faster as well as bigger, saving steps, proper footwork and court positioning become more important. Having players chasing after balls or running helter-skelter generally leads to poor percentage play. Having your setter in a position to play the pass more easily and to play it with more time and less effort will save many points over a season.

Tim Davison is the girls' volleyball coach at Selah High School in Selah, Wash., and is a USA Volleyball CAP certified coach.

Section VIII: How to Develop Drills

The effective volleyball coach will plan practices that maximize team performance in match situations. Essential to that end is the integration of four key ingredients into drill development. Drills must be:

1) goal-oriented
2) integrated
3) continuous
4) pressure-packed.

This essay will discuss each concept in depth and give concrete examples of how they may be incorporated into volleyball drill design.

GOAL-ORIENTED DRILLS

In an effort to challenge the players, keep them motivated and help them reach their potential, it is important to structure the drills so that a goal must be met before they end. Time is an artificial goal. A drill which requires players to perform a skill for a time often results in poor performance and lack of concentration. Rather, specific goals must be established to keep the players focused on the skills being drilled. Ways to structure goal-oriented drills include incorporating a variety of scoring systems in drill construction:

1) repetition
2) time/repetition/percentage
3) plus/minus
4) wash.

Repetition as a scoring system involves establishing the total number of perfect repetitions that must be performed, either by the individual or team. The coach may also challenge players in a consecutive repetition drill where an error results in starting the drill over. An example of the repetition scoring system would be a drill which requires each player to serve five consecutive serves to the No. 5 position. Similarly, the coach may set the goal based on time/repetition/percentage. For example, a drill may require an individual or team to pass seven out of 10 balls perfectly, or 70% in five minutes or 30 good passes in five minutes.

The plus/minus scoring method allows positive points (+1, +2, +3) to be awarded if a skill is executed well and deducts points if the skill is executed incorrectly or missed.

The following is an example of the plus/minus scoring system for a hitting drill:

◆ Each individual or team would be awarded +2 points for a line hit, +1 for cross-court hit, O for hits to other areas and -1 for missed or out-of-bounds hits.

◆ Game is 15 points.

The wash principle establishes a goal to reach, where several consecutive steps are necessary to get there. If the skills are not performed consecutively, everything is a wash and the player or team starts over. Wash drills emphasize a very important part of the game of volleyball: Players must work toward achieving one point at a time and the game is not over until it is over.

An example of a wash drill with six on six scrimmage is as follows:

Photo: Notre Dame

According to Knortz, in order for players to perform well in matches, practices must also be gamelike.

According to Hurley and Mills (1993), "so often, we tell our athletes how important the outcome of a certain match or competition is to the team, to us as coaches and how important it should be to the athletes themselves. Little do we know that the amount of "importance" that an athlete places on an event can be far greater than what we expected." As a result, coaches must ask themselves the following questions:

1. Do I motivate my athletes using fear?

2. When critiquing an athlete's performance, do I focus on the performance (a specific behavior) or do I place a value judgment on the athlete?

3. Are all of my team and individual goals outcome-oriented or process-oriented?

4. Have I ever implied to my athletes that they are worthless? Have I ever implied this even after my most frustrating moments as a coach?

5. Is there enough trust between the athletes and myself for them to feel that they can take personal risks?

6. How do I treat my athlete(s) after constant mistakes/errors, a career ending injury, upon quitting the team, retirement or being cut from the team?"

(Hurley, Erin and Brett Mills. Examining self-acceptance: a new approach to performance. *Coaching Volleyball*, June/July 1993, 22-23.)

142

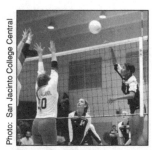

The coach must drill the game as a whole rather than isolating pieces of the game.

◆ The object of the drill is to complete all six rotations before the other team completes a rotation.
◆ Each team earns the right to rotate by winning two rallies in a row.
◆ Two rallies include a serve rally and a free ball rally.
◆ Team A receives the serve and the rally is played.
◆ One team must win both rallies in order to rotate.

Often the terms little point/big point are used. If the first rally is won, the winning team scores a little point. When both rallies are won, the winning team scores a big point and rotates.

When practicing the first team against the second, there are ways to handicap the drill to ensure a challenge. The coach may require the first team to get two big points to rotate, versus one big point for the second team. Another way to handicap the first team is to require them always to serve and the second team always to receive the free ball. This challenges the first team always to win its points on defense.

INTEGRATED DRILLS

When constructing the drills they should have a game-like quality. Players should pass from back court toward the net, be positioned in standard defensive positions when drilling defensive systems and the drill should be initiated off a pass rather than a coach's toss.

In order to maximize team success, it is essential to train in an integrated manner or with game-like quality. In doing so, the coach drills the game as a whole, rather than isolating pieces of the game. When players are in the learning phase they are often drilled in a very controlled manner. Often partner drills or coach-initiated drills are used at this stage. As soon as possible, the coach should move on to combination drills, where two or more additional skills are added to help provide more feedback.

Essential to this concept is attention to the use of the court and net, positions of players and sequence of movement. When constructing the drills they should have a game-like quality. Players should pass from back court toward the net, be positioned in standard defensive positions when drilling defensive systems and the drill should be initiated off a pass rather than a coach's toss.

The following is an example of an integrated drill:
◆ The coach continually serves the balls to a designated receiver.
◆ The setter sets off the pass and hitters (in all three front-row positions) hit the set. (This drill allows for imperfections of preceding skills, which will occur in the game situation.)
◆ The setter must learn to set imperfect passes and the hitters must learn to hit imperfect sets.
◆ The hitters gain practice hitting out of all three positions, or if specializing, gain extensive practice in one position.
◆ To add the concept of "goal-oriented" the coach should set a goal that must be achieved before the drill ends.

CONTINUOUS DRILLS

The concept of continuous requires drill construction be designed to increase the number of ball contacts, physically condition players while working on skills and allow no time for players to dwell on mistakes. An example of a continuous drill is continuous rotation triples.

In a three vs. three rally, if an error occurs, the coach gives the player the ball in the same manner it came to him/her prior to the error. This allows the player to repeat the skill and practice those skills that need more work. If a player does not go for the ball, he/she is asked to show how they should have gone for the ball and then given another ball to play. Once team members successfully put the ball over the net, they rotate off quickly and a new team rotates in from the endline. The goal could be 15 pass-set-hit combinations.

Enhancing team performance is easy if drills are pressure-packed and game-like.

PRESSURE-PACKED DRILLS

Pressure-packed drills place the player or team under conditions that simulate pressure situations encountered during matches. They push the players to a psychological and physiological limit. They may create tension and anxiety in order to teach a player to cope. In addition, they help develop a team philosophy, attitude and create mental toughness.

The concept of pressure can be introduced to drills by several methods. A coach may ask the practice official to call one team tightly and the other loosely. Or they may award a point or call an error during the drill based on an erroneous judgment. The players must learn to deal with poor officiating calls or when things do not go their way.

Pressure can be added by placing a "penalty" on teams when errors occur or when they lose the drill. This provides for increased motivation, and keeps levels of concentration and intensity high. Care should be taken to ensure the penalty is not perceived as a punishment. This can be accomplished by keeping it light. For example, the penalty may be for the losers to bring water to the winners.

Wash drills emphasize a very important part of the game of volleyball: players must work toward achieving one point at a time and the game is not over until it is over. Pressure can also be manufactured by placing the team in critical situations such as match point, tied at 12-12 or serving at 12-14. If it is expected that the players do perform well under pressure, the coach must work hard to incorporate this element into the practice drills.

In conclusion, it is the coach who develops drills that are goal-oriented, game-like and continuous, with the element of pressure in practice who will be rewarded by enhanced team performance. Individual creativity will allow the coach to decide what the team needs to achieve and construct drills that work toward that goal.

By integrating the four major concepts into drill construction, the team will be better prepared for match competition. The reason is clear: The players have been challenged consistently throughout practices which were designed to be as game-like as possible.

Geri Knortz is the head women's volleyball coach at Hamilton College in Clinton, N.Y., and is a USA Volleyball CAP certified coach.

According to Hebert (1994), high school and junior level officials are far too severe in their decisions about when to stop play for a ball handling violation.

"Sound educational theory tells us that athletes in their formative stages need to be given greater latitude in their attemps to execute skills. As they develop through higher levels of play, they can be judged by a more demanding set of officiating standards. Youngsters learn better where there is positive reinforcement. Negative reinforcement which is too severe can only retard the learning process."

(Hebert, Mike. A coach takes a look at volleyball officiating. *Coaching Volleyball*, March 1994, 18-21.)

Developing Drills

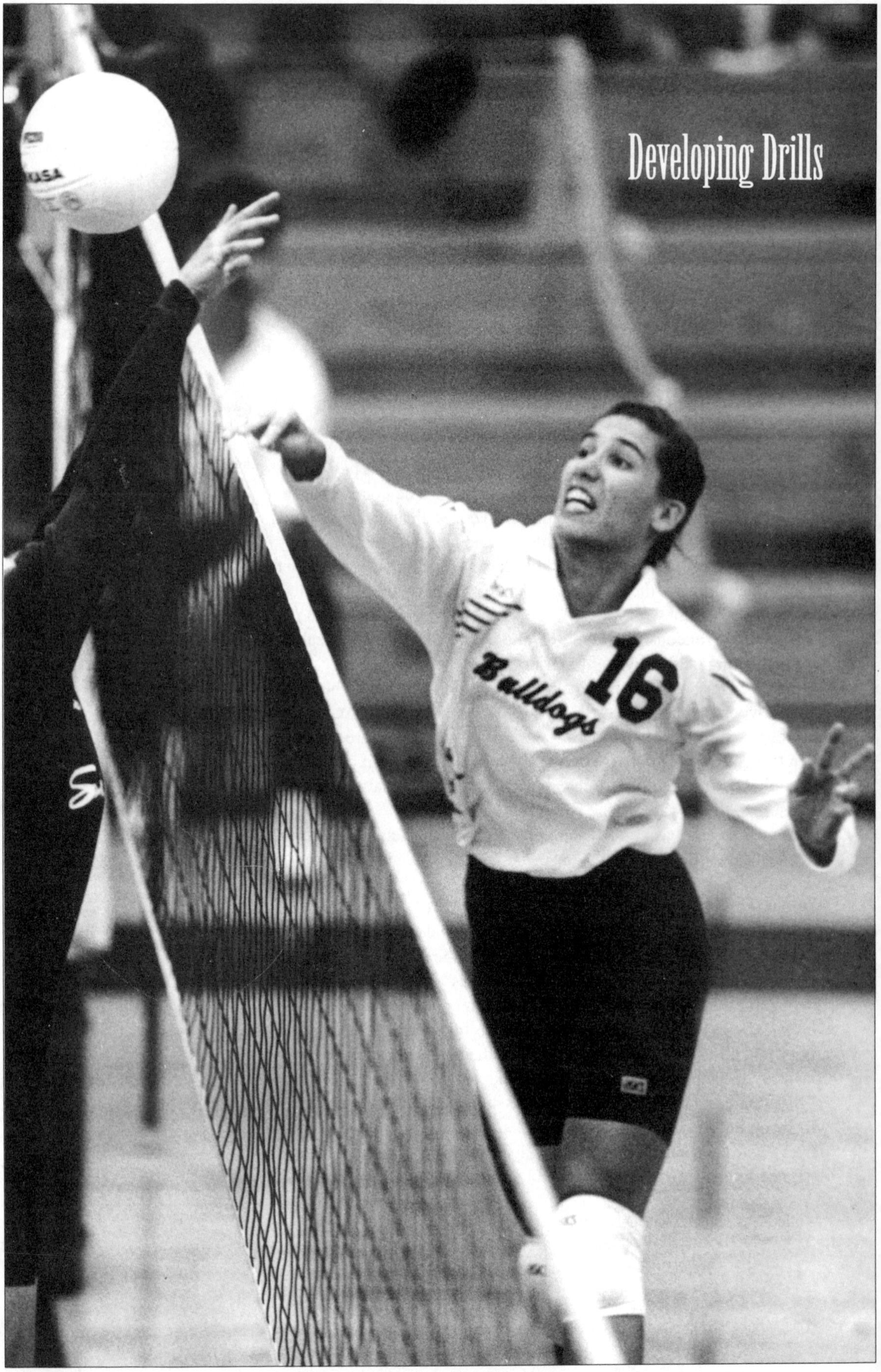

Developing Drills

ZEN GOLEMBIOWSKY AND
PETER JOHN STEFANIUK

145

To prepare a team properly for competition, a coach must develop drills that enable players to learn and refine their individual and team skills. Factors that a coach must address when developing successful drills include team drill behavior, team readiness, preparation, pace, intensity and combinations.

Coaches must teach effective team drill behavior in practice for players to come away with skills they can use in a match.

TEAM DRILL BEHAVIOR

Team drill behavior is not something players bring to a program; it is a responsibility that must be learned. Drills are a function of the entire team. The coach and players in a drill are not the only people involved. There is a role for everyone—feeders, shaggers, safety people and encouragers. Prevent your players from being casual observers or chitchatting during drills. Total team involvement during drills:

- reduces the possibility of drill breakdown
- provides for a safer training environment
- enhances learning through observation
- helps prevent cooldown and
- fosters team unity.

TEAM READINESS

Developing drills that progress from lead-up to advanced for each fundamental skill and aspect of volleyball should be an ongoing process in your coaching career. Select drills compatible with your players' abilities so they can experience success as they train. Use your judgment to decide when to progress to the next degree of difficulty. A 50% success factor is a good indicator that your players are ready to advance to the next level.

A coach should never come to practice unprepared. She or he should have goals, performance objectives and behavioral changes in mind when structuring a practice.

PRACTICE PREPARATION

A coach should never come to practice unprepared. She or he should have goals, performance objectives and behavioral changes in mind when structuring a practice. The following are examples:

Goals

1. Players will serve/receive 25 balls.
2. Spikers will hit 20 minutes against a two-person block.

Performance Objectives

1. Player will stay in drill until 10 balls are successfully passed to a target.
2. Team will serve 15 balls consecutively without an error.

Behavioral Changes

1. Problem behavior—Players do not communicate while serving/receiving.

Behavioral change drill—Receiving player yells "mine" during team reception drills.

2. Problem behavior—Spikers hit only crosscourt shots in competition.

Photo: Scott Quintard

According to the authors, to reach a higher sports form your players need to practice drills that require maximum physical effort.

Behavioral change drill—Spikers work on hitting down the line in practice. Explain drill objectives to your players so they understand what they are working to achieve each session.

PACE

In good practice sessions, the drills follow a rhythmic pace, avoiding long delays that cause boredom, cool-down or lapses in concentration. A breakdown in pace can result from:

❏ delays between drills caused by poor organization
❏ latecomers
❏ slow moving players
❏ long water breaks
❏ lengthy explanations
❏ lack of desire
❏ fatigue or boredom.

You can improve the pace of your practices by eliminating any of the problems mentioned and by:

❏ involving your manager and assistant coach in leading drills
❏ using more than one court
❏ shagging balls immediately
❏ using a whistle for communication and
❏ playing lively music.

INTENSITY

To reach a higher "sports form," your players need to practice drills that require maximum physical effort. These special high-intensity drills should occur at least twice in a daily session, once

The coach should be aware of the levels of physical output required by various parts of practice and how to balance those variables for the players' benefit.

for offense and once for defense. High intensity drills help a team find its fighting spirit and help the players discover how much effort they are capable of. Two samples include:

Offense

A player spikes 10 consecutive balls, moving quickly back to the 10-foot line after each hit.

Defense

A player digs 10 balls tossed randomly around the court.

The coach should be aware of the levels of physical output required by various parts of practice and how to balance those variables for the players' benefit. Intensity should be raised and lowered intentionally throughout practice to accommodate for fatigue and the drill sequence should allow for maximum utilization of warm muscles.

Spiking is better than a ball control drill after a hard warmup; serving can be used as an arm warmup for spiking and vice versa; setting drills should not immediately follow pushups; intensity drills should be followed by a water break.

In a weekly plan, the coach should vary the intensity patterns of drills from day to day.

COMBINATIONS

As players develop, combination drills that use several fundamentals will help players transfer skills to game situations. It is not enough to practice digging, spiking, setting and so on in isolated drills. At some point you must train players to perform skills in full game sequences.

The analysis of player movement patterns on the court is the foundation of drill structure and the concept underlying combination drills. When a coach can see the various combinations of player movements in each rotation, she or he begins to be freed from relying on someone else's drill book.

SAMPLE COMBINATION DRILL
◆ Pass and set
◆ Pass, set, spike
◆ Pass, set, spike, cover
◆ Pass, set, spike, cover, back to defense or block and turn toward court
◆ Block, turn, play a ball
◆ Block, turn, play ball, come off net for spike approach
◆ Serve, move to defense
◆ Serve, move to defense, dig ball
◆ Serve, move to defense, dig ball, cover.

Zen Golembiowsky is a volleyball coach from Hinckley, Ohio. Peter John Stefaniuk is a volleyball coach from Toronto, Ontario, Canada.

Training Volleyball Skills With Game-Oriented Drills

HORST BAACKE

149

Baacke believes each drill should present a problem to be solved, derived from a corresponding game situation.

Modern, high-level volleyball requires a mastery of playing skills. However, skill mastery cannot be achieved with old-fashioned, simple, abstract technique drills that are isolated from the tactics of play and the variability of game situations. Players have to learn to perfect skills in accordance with the requirements of the game and as a complex unit of tactical decisions, technical and physical execution and mental involvement. The following illustrates the relationship between game situations and individual skills.

GAME SITUATION
- ◆ perceiving of information
  - ▲ flight of ball
  - ▲ positions and actions of teammates and opponents
  - ▲ own position, posture, movement, muscle perception

MAKING A DECISION
- ◆ evaluating the situation
  - ▲ processing of information
  - ▲ comprehending the situation
  - ▲ remembering former experiences from training or matches
- ◆ anticipation
- ◆ electing a tactical solution
  - ▲ according to former experiences
  - ▲ according to (fixed) team patterns (team system)
  - ▲ new decisions (creativity)
- ◆ selecting an appropriate technique

TECHNIQUE PERFORMANCE
- ◆ give feedback on control of action concerning correct movement, quality, reactions of opponents and teammates; make corrections

RESULT OF ACTION
- ◆ give feedback on the evaluation of the result in regard to the proposed corrections

NEW GAME SITUATION
The following are principles and methodical hints for selecting or building appropriate drills, mainly for players who have already learned the basic techniques.

GAMELIKE TASKS
Each drill or exercise should present a problem to be solved, derived from a corresponding (or slightly simplified) game situation. The solution to the problem has to be well carried out by an appropriate action (technical realization) in the drill. The players have to perform their actions tactically, as well as technically, according to the game situation

150

(Note: The setter is Player 3 and Player 6 is up.)

Figure 1: The ball is served to the receiver, who passes to the setter, who sets either hitter.

Figure 2: The coach throws the ball to the receiver, who passes to the setter. The receiver then covers behind the outside hitter as the setter sets that hitter. The receiver rotates to the end of the line and the next player becomes the receiver.

Figure 3: The coach serves to the receiver, who passes to the setter. The receiver then covers behind the outside hitter as the setter sets that hitter who has taken the correct approach to the net.

Figure 4: The same as Figure 3 except the setter also covers behind the hitter and the hitter actually spikes the ball.

Figure 5: The coach serves to the receiver, who passes to the setter, who sets the outside hitter. The outside hitter spikes the ball and a second coach tosses the ball over to simulate a blocked ball; all players must be in position to cover as shown.

Figure 6: The ball is served to the receiver. The receiver passes to the setter, who sets the outside hitter, who spikes the ball. The coach, on a platform at the net, tosses the ball to simulate a block, which the players must cover as indicated.

Progression Drill For Service Reception - Figures 1-6

DIAGRAM SYMBOLS

Coach	⊗
Main Action Player	⊙
Other Players	○△
Ball Feeder	⊘
Blocking Palyer	Ω
Path of the Ball	—→
Spiked Ball	----→
Path of a Player	·····→
Ball Box	□
Platform	▭

(See Figures 1 and 2.)

GAMELIKE POSITIONING AND MOVEMENT

Drills should be carried out on the court with the correct spacing in relation to the net and with the positioning and movement of the players corresponding to the game situation. In this way, players learn and become accustomed to their positions and movement on the court— they get the feeling for space and distances, for the net and lines (see Figures 3 and 4, 7 and 8).

MAIN ACTION IN THE CENTER

Drills should comprise one main action that solves the problem according to the game situation. The attention of the players and the coach is concentrated first and foremost on this action. All the other actions of the drill have to support the correct execution of the main action—high quality on it is essential (see Figures 2-6, 8-11).

GAMELIKE CHAIN OF ACTIONS

The main action should be a link in a chain of actions, as in a game. Drills should include at least one action preceding and one action following the main action (thus, a gamelike chain). We consider the preceding and the following action under two aspects—according to the player who performs the main actions (who has to perform his or her preceding and following action) and according to the team. We also consider the actions without and with the ball. (It is very important to teach the actions without the ball according to the real game situations together with the skills.) (see Figures 3-6, 9-12).

GAMELIKE DYNAMICS AND SPEED

Players have to execute skills in a drill with the same speed, agility and dynamics as in a game. They must perform the main action, in particular, as quickly and dynamically as in a game. Modern play is very fast and dynamic and players have to get used to it in training. Position, posture and motion should correspond to the fast changing situations. Move to the ball, execute the skill, cover the court by quick movements and shifting.

(Note: The setter is Player 3 and Player 6 is up.)

Figure 7: The coach spikes the ball to the retriever, who passes to the setter.

Figure 8: The coach spikes the ball to the retriever, who passes to the setter. The setter sets the outside hitter as the retriever moves into position behind the hitter. A middle back player is ready to retrieve an errant pass.

Figure 9: The coach spikes the ball from a platform to the retriever, who passes the ball to the setter, who sets the outside hitter, who has made the correct approach to the net. Both the setter and retriever move into correct position to cover behind the hitter.

Figure 10: The coach on the platform spikes the ball to the retriever, who passes the ball to the setter, who sets the outside hitter, who spikes the ball. The setter and retriever move into position to cover behind the hitter and a second coach at the net tosses the ball over to simulate a block.

Figure 11: The setter is in position to block as the coach on the platform spikes the ball to the retriever. The setter then gets into position to receive the pass from the retriever. The setter sets the outside hitter, who spikes the ball. Players get into correct coverage position as shown.

Figure 12: The setter is in blocking position as the coach on the platform spikes the ball to the retriever. The setter gets into position and receives the pass from the retriever. The setter sets the outside hitter, who spikes the ball. All players move into correct coverage positions and the coach on the platform tosses the ball over to simulate a block.

Figure 13: Two blockers are in position at the net as shown; the coach on the platform spikes the ball to the left back player, who passes the ball to the setter, who has moved into position. The setter sets the outside hitter, who spikes the ball against a two-player block; the setter and the left back player should be in correct coverage positions.

Figure 14: Players are positioned as shown; the coach sets the hitter, who spikes against a block; back-row players retrieve.

Figure 15: The coach set the hitter, who either spikes or tips against the block. Back-row players position themselves to cover spike, tip or deflection off the block.

Progression Drill For Retreiving - Figures 7-15

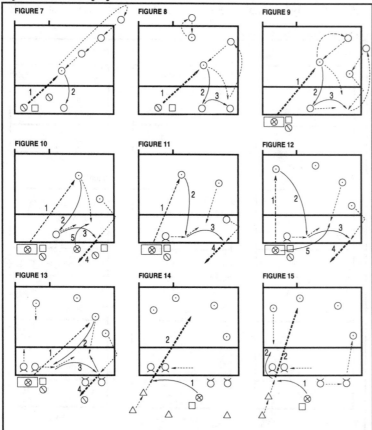

Figure 16: The coach tosses the ball to the back-row player, who passes to the setter.

Figure 17: The coach throws the ball over the net to the back-row player, who passes to the setter, who sets the hitter.

Figure 18: The coach throws the ball to the left back player, who passes to the setter who sets the hitter. The left back player gets into position to cover behind the hitter, then rotates to the end of the line. The coach tosses a ball to the right back player, who passes to the setter, who sets the hitter. The right back player covers behind the hitter.

Figure 19: The coach throws the ball slightly away from the middle back player, who moves to the ball and passes the ball to the setter, who sets the left outside hitter. The middle back player covers behind the hitter and then rotates to the end of the line as the next player moves up into the middle back position. The procedure is followed again, this time to the other side, as shown.

Figure 20: The coach throws the ball so the middle back player has to go back to retrieve it. The middle back player passes the ball to the setter, who sets either outside hitter.

Figure 21: This time the coach throws the ball so the middle back player has to move back to one of the corners to retrieve it. The middle back player again passes to the setter, who sets an outside hitter as shown.

Figure 22: The coach throws the ball to the left back player, who passes to the setter who sets the hitter. The left back covers behind the hitter.

Figure 23: The coach throws the ball to the middle back player, who passes to either outside hitter. The left and right back players cover behind the spike. The coach then tosses another ball simulating a blocked ball.

Figure 24: The coach throws the ball to the right back player, who passes to the setter, who sets the left outside hitter who spikes the ball. The left back player and the setter have moved in to cover behind the block.

GAMELIKE COOPERATION

Drills should require (at least for the main action) a gamelike cooperation and communication of the players involved concerning preparation, positioning, communication, assistance, animation, covering and so on. The players have to acquire a "blind understanding" in their cooperation—this must be practiced (see Figures 3-6, 8 and 9, 11 and 12).

ACTIVE OR PASSIVE OPPONENT

Drills should include an opponent, either active or passive, as far as it corresponds to the game situation. In the real match, nearly all game situations are influenced by the opponent's actions or reactions. The chain of actions starts with an opponent's action and may also end with it. In a drill the opponent may be replaced or simulated by the teammates or the coach (see Figures 2-6, 8-15, 25-28).

VARIETY

Drills should be performed variably, corresponding with the game situation—no mechanical, schematic repetition of the same motion. Players should adapt their actions to the variety of game situations—technically as well as tactically, mentally and physically. Drills should develop the "ability to play," to make decisions, to change over very fast, to adapt

Progression Drill For Passing After a Free Ball - Figures 16-24

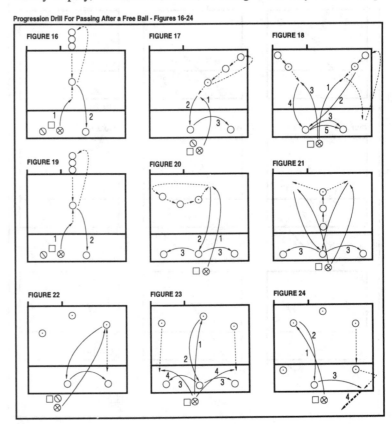

Progression Drill For Quick Sequence - Figures 25-28B

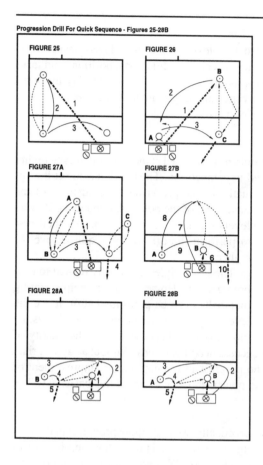

FIGURE 25 FIGURE 26

FIGURE 27A FIGURE 27B

FIGURE 28A FIGURE 28B

Figure 25: The coach spikes from a platform and Players A and B alternate retrieving and setting.

Figure 26: The coach spikes from the platform, Player A blocks and sets and Players B and C alternate retrieving and spiking.

Figures 27A and 27B: The coach spikes from a platform and Players A and B alternate retrieving and setting. Players C and D alternate spiking.

Figure 28A: The coach on platform spikes (1) and throws (2), Player A blocks and retrieves, Player B sets and Player A spikes.

Figure 28B: Same as 28A, except Players A and B change tasks.

action to the situation and to be mentally mobile (see Figures 9,11 and 12, 15).

COMPLEXITY

Drills should be arranged so, at least for the main action, the complex character of the skills is guaranteed as concerns the unity of the four components (tactical, mental, technical and physical). It is possible (and often advisable) to stress one of the components more or less, but not by neglecting the others. Especially for learning new skills, we first pay attention to correct technical execution. If we emphasize the tactical or physical aspect of a skill, we never should allow bad technique.

CONTROL OF THE RESULT - (FEEDBACK)

A drill should include a clear goal in accordance with the game situation. The result of the actions should be easily evaluated or controlled by the players themselves. Technical and tactical quality of the actions improves with feedback and immediate correction. Control of results gives better motivation for correct performance. The feedback is supported by the criticisms of the coach (see Figures 2-6, 9, 12, 15).

PLAYER ROLES

Drills should be related to the roles of the players. Players' tasks should be set in conformity with their specialized functions, positions and tasks in the team play. This way, as many players as possible play the same roles as in the game. This is especially important for the players who have to perform the main action of a drill.

QUALITY OF PLAY

The actions of drills should be performed at the same or an even higher level of quality as required in competition. The coach has to set the appropriate criteria for the quality of the actions and the outcome of the drill, based on the performance level of the potential opponents. Players should know the expected level of quality for each drill and do their best to perform the drill at the required level or higher.

Without an appropriate level of quality there is no progress in training and no improvement of performance. Coaches and players must be aware of this basic "law."

These principles are mainly related to drill organization. However, the principle stating that drills must be performed at or above the level of quality required in competition is the most essential because it rules the quality of training and determining success in competitions. Without an appropriate level of quality there is no progress in training and no improvement of performance. Coaches and players must be aware of this basic "law."

PROGRESSION DRILLS

To use these principles practically, we may apply progression drills— a succession of drills starting very simple and proceeding step-by-step to more complicated and game-like drills. We derive such a set of progression drills from a game situation or from a fragment of the game.

We use a simplified drill at the beginning of the succession, which corresponds to our players' actual potential (in regard to all four components of the playing action). That means we start with a drill that can be performed with good quality by the weakest player. Then between the first and the last drill we include all the intermediate steps necessary to reach the final goal and to lead the players to the intended mastery of the selected skill or game situation, respectively (see Figures 1-24).

Each step of a progression must be done in accordance to this principle: As simple as necessary, as game-like as possible.

The drills of each step are repeated and varied until the players perfect the drill. The criterion for mastery in each drill is the quality of the main action in regard to its technical and tactical performance and in regard to the game. We do not proceed to the next drill until players have fulfilled the criteria of the previous one.

In each training session, we briefly repeat all of the previously practiced drills of the sequence (or at least the last few) before we start the main drill of the session.

CONCENTRATION

To learn, improve, stabilize and perfect mastery of a playing action requires thousands of repetitions and months of time. Therefore, we recommend emphasizing one or two skills for a longer time and practicing one drill (eventually with some variants) for 30 to 90 minutes each training session; that means 50,000, or more repetitions for the main action (advanced players may do even more). But simple repetition is not sufficient. Only the number of tactical and technically correct repetitions are essential—otherwise we stabilize something incorrectly or prolong considerably the time required for mastery.

QUALITY OVER QUANTITY

If we take too much time to develop one or two skills, we do not leave enough time to improve the other elements of the game. Therefore, we take the rest of the time to preserve the attained level of play (see Figures 1-24).

ACTIVE ROLE OF THE COACH

The process of learning and improving playing actions can be faster and more effective if the coach or an assistant works actively with players during the drills. The coach can especially influence the quality of practices through:
- correct execution of the drill
- correct execution of the main action
- appropriate solution to the tactical problem
- variations of the task and their execution
- motivation, mobilization and stimulation of the players
- control, feedback and correction. The coach should actively take part in the practice session, not only verbally but also practically.

Horst Baacke is a Federation Internationale de Volleyball (FIVB) technical advisor located in Sundern, Germany.

Games That Teach the Drive
and Wipe-Off Shots

Games That Teach the Drive and Wipe-Off Shots

Don Shondell

Most beginning volleyball players either try to avoid the block completely or conservatively pull the ball down into the block, often resulting in an attack error. To avoid this, your players should learn two specific shots—the drive and the wipe-off. The drive shot is hit at the blocker's upper fingers above the most distal joint, causing an upward deflection that sends the ball slightly upward and far beyond the baseline of the court. The wipe-off shot, especially the outside wipe-off, is one that can be used to win instant points. The player rotates the hitting arm at the last instant, hitting or pushing the ball into the outside half of the outside hand of the outside blocker. This shot is seldom returned because it is hit away from the court with a quick deflection. An inside wipe-off shot can also be used, but this shot can be played up by the drop-off blocker. To allow each player to concentrate meaningfully on the drive and wipe-off shots, use competitive games that emphasize these specific skills. Competitive games create more sincere attempts to do things correctly than do the normal noncompetitive drills. These games also allow players to practice blocking and digging these two shots.

According to Shondell, competitive games create more sincere attempts to do things correctly than do the normal noncompetitive drills.

EQUIPMENT

Use a narrow volleyball court (30 feet deep on each side of the net and 15 feet wide) for this game. A line parallel to and 15 feet from the sideline is taped from baseline to baseline. An antenna is placed in the middle of the net to help mark the divided courts. Two games can be played on a regulation volleyball court.

RULES

• The server must serve strong, making the single defender move at least one step to make the pass. The rationale is that with advanced players it is important to stress ball placement and control. The penalty for a server's failure to make the receiver move at least one step is loss of serve.

• Only one person may pass. This creates a situation in which one player receives practice in covering half the court. The penalty for anyone besides the single deep receiver passing the ball is a point for the server.

• The attacking rule is that the attacker must hit off the block on every attempted shot unless he or she hits between a block that has not properly closed. No soft shots or tips are permitted. The exception to this rule is for defensive saves that cannot be controlled and are returned across the net. Over-passes may be hit directly to the floor. Any controlled hit that passes outside the blocker but is not touched by the blocker is considered an error even though it lands in the court. This forces the attacker to go for the hands.

• To allow all players to work on all skills, players should rotate from left front to right front to back row. The left front is the attacker, the right front is the setter and the center back is the server, passer and deep position digger. To facilitate hitting off the block, the setter should set the ball into the center of the court area, at least 2 feet from the net. The rationale for this game-like drill is that it provides all players practice at each of the volleyball skills of serving, passing, setting, digging, attacking and blocking in a meaningful competitive situation. The drill might be modified to allow a setter to specialize if so desired.

VARIATIONS

• The game may be played to 11 or 15 points.

• Blockers may not pull their hands down against wipe-off or drive shots.

• To emphasize covering the spiker, both the setter and the back-row player must call "cover" and cover the hitter. You could make it a rule that a point or side-out is awarded to the other team if the setter and back-row player do not cover as stated.

• The center back should remain near the baseline and dig balls driven off the top of the block or take a step in and dig balls hit through the block. The blockers should replay any deflections between the net and the 3-meter line.

Don Shondell, Ph.D., is the head men's volleyball coach at Ball State University in Muncie, Ind.

Three-Person and
Nine-Person Pepper

Three-Person Pepper

STEVE DeBOER

Volleyball is a unique sport in that you have a number of very different skills which each player must be able to do well to be good. There is the forearm pass (bump/dig), the overhead pass (set) and the attack (a topspin overhand hit). In executing these skills, the more control you use, the better off you will be.

Probably the simplest and most effective drill/game to practice all of these skills while working on control is the game of Pepper, where two players pass-set-hit the ball back and forth amongst themselves. I often refer to the game as Controlled Pepper with younger players, emphasizing that they should not just "bat" the ball around.

Pepper is fantastic for working on individual skills while keeping the ball in play. It can also be an exciting and challenging game for players as they work to keep the rally going longer each time. There is one major flaw in this game, however, when you think of volleyball on the court: you do not want to dig the ball back to the person who just attacked it, as they are usually on the other side of the net. Instead, you want to dig the ball to your setter. This is where the game of Three Person Pepper comes in handy.

Traditional pepper, enhanced by the addition of one more player, is a fantastic way to work on individual skills.

In Three Person Pepper, two of the players are designated as hitters/diggers, with the third being the setter. The diggers will always pass the ball to the setter; the setter will set the ball back to them; and they will then attack the ball to the other player who passes the ball to the setter and then prepares to attack. The key to remember is that the setter always sets the person who just passed them the ball. Following the figure to the right, B passes to A; A sets to B; B attacks to C; C passes to A; A sets to C; C attacks to B, etc. Again, your players will be constantly working on their individual skills while controlling the ball to keep the rally going.

Both Two-Person and Three-Person Pepper have their benefits. We use one or the other, if not both, everyday in practice. Good luck as you work with your players to develop not only their skills, but also their interest in the sport of volleyball.

Steve DeBoer is the former assistant women's volleyball coach at the College of William & Mary. He now lives in Columbus, Ohio, and is a USA Volleyball CAP certified coach.

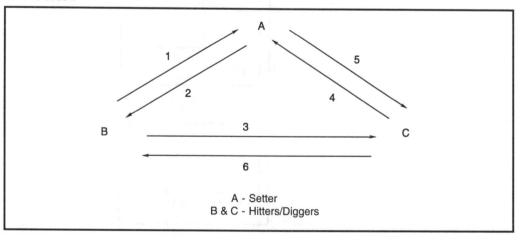

A - Setter
B & C - Hitters/Diggers

Nine-Person Pepper

We developed this drill for five reasons: To condition the setter, to practice attacking from a variety of places and positions, to practice defense behind a single blocker, to improve back-row attack and digging abilities and to provide a competitive drill that involves all of the skills.

Nine-Player Pepper uses nine (or more) players, including at least one setter. The coach initiates a free or down ball to one side of the net. The setter takes that side and sets attackers with either a high front, a high back or a back-row set.

All attackers may hit. The opposing team may have one blocker on the front row attacks but must dig the back row attacks. After setting the ball the setter crosses under the net (if your setter is not very mobile, use two) and sets the same four sets in transition for the other team. The rally continues with the setter setting for both sides until a mistake is made or a kill is scored.

Then the coach initiates a free or down ball to the other team and a rally ensues. If a team wins both rallies, it scores a point. The first team to score two points gets to rotate. If the two teams split the rally series, no points are scored.

The team that rotates first through all four positions wins. Every time a team rotates, the score for both teams goes back to zero, beginning a new game.

VARIATIONS

• If your hitters are very accomplished at scoring against a single blocker you may require your setter to set all balls 5 to 7 feet from the net.

• If your team is not very accomplished at hitting or blocking you may want all four players in the back court digging.

Kathy DeBoer is the associate athletic director at the University of Kentucky and is a USA Volleyball CAP certified coach.

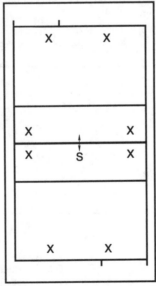